UNDEPRESSED

A Comprehensive Guide to Understanding, Managing, and Overcoming Depression

WALEED Mahmud

Other Books by the Author

<u>Probing Freewill</u>: A Story of Autonomy & Inevitability

<u>This is NOT Education</u>: Rethinking the Education System

<u>Power & Ethics</u>: A Brief History of Western Moral and Political Philosophy

<u>Decrypting Globalization</u>: Understanding the Economic, Cultural, And Political afflictions of Nationalism, Migration and the Environmental Crisis

Follow on Medium:

https://medium.com/@waleedmtariq

Follow on SubStack:

https://waleedmahmud.substack.com/

Follow on Instagram:
https://www.instagram.com/waleedmtariq/

Copyright © 2024 Waleed Mahmud Tariq

All rights reserved.

ASIN: B0D8HMK7T6

A Sonnet of Hope

You possess your soul, ever striving to appease,
A heart that seeks solace, a mind yearning for peace
In this world of acrimony, within my nostalgic dreams,
I find comfort in whispers, where moonlight softly gleams.

The days of yore, with gentle grace, in memory reside,
Where joy and sorrow intertwine, like waves upon the tide.
Amidst the chaos of the now, a beacon bright and pure,
Guides me back to simpler times, where love could still endure.

Yet time marches on, relentless and indifferent to our plea,
It carries us from our cherished past, to what we cannot see.
But in the quiet of the night, when stars begin to shine,
I wander through my reveries, and make the past align.

With heart in hand, I face the endless night,
And seek the dawn, to find my way to light.

Waleed Mahmud

Dedicated to

My incredible family, whose unwavering support and love have been my anchor through the stormiest of times. Your belief in me has been a constant source of strength and inspiration.

To my beloved spouse, whose patience, understanding, and endless encouragement have made this journey possible. Your love has been my guiding light, illuminating the path even in the darkest moments.

Thank you for standing by my side, for your sacrifices, and for your unyielding faith in my dreams. This book is as much yours as it is mine.

TABLE OF CONTENTS

"If we start being honest about our pain, our anger and our shortcomings instead of pretending they don't exist, then maybe we'll leave the world a better place than we found it."

-

Russell Wilson

PREFACE

When I was in my early teens, I felt a relentless sense of disconnection. It wasn't just the typical teenage angst; it was deeper, darker. I had an existential crisis before I even knew what the term meant. Imagine this: a kid who should be carefree, worrying about school crushes and weekend plans, instead pondering the meaning of life and death. I felt like an alien on this planet, always yearning for a place that seemed out of reach, perhaps even non-existent.

I tried to change everything about myself to escape this void. I switched hairstyles, adopted new dress senses, but nothing worked. No matter what I did, I couldn't shake the feeling that I didn't belong. That's when I turned to books—philosophy, religion, spirituality, science—anything that promised answers. I vividly remember reading "***The Power of Now***" by Eckhart Tolle. It was a revelation. For the first time, I encountered the idea that happiness and contentment come from within, not from the external world. Yet, even as these insights resonated with me, my depression gnawed at my core, influencing every decision I made.

I was always good at intellectual pursuits. School subjects came naturally to me. Science, math, literature, poetry; you name it. But while I excelled academically, I struggled to keep my mind in check. In my early twenties, I finally sought help from a psychologist. I remember sitting in her office, feeling isolated from the world, resentful that I had to pay someone to have this conversation because no one else seemed willing to talk openly about these feelings.

One particularly painful memory is of a hospital visit. The receptionist whispered "psychiatrist" as if it were a dirty word. The stigma was palpable. The first time I used a scalpel to cut my wrists, I didn't know what I was doing. I just wanted the pain to stop. I was found messy and bloody, and rushed over by family with a desperate urgency, unsure of what to do. I remember being terrified of my parents' reaction, expecting judgment and anger. Fortunately, that didn't happen, but the fact that I feared it speaks volumes about the stigma surrounding mental health.

Over the years, I've faced more than my fair share of dark moments. There were times when I overdosed on benzodiazepines, hoping to just sleep and never wake up. When I was found, I was dragged to the hospital, and woke up groggy and ashamed. It's hard for families to cope with this. It's a nightmare for them, and I get why some people might see these actions as selfish. But people need to understand that no one wants to hurt themselves. It's not cowardice; it's desperation.

The first time I tried to write a suicide note, I cried myself to sleep. The paper was soaked with tears because I couldn't bear the thought of hurting my parents and family. I remember how it started with a single cut, giving me a sense of control, and then it evolved into a ritual of self-harm. The euphoria, the temporary escape from the pain of depression, was addictive. During therapy, my doctor suggested Electroconvulsive Therapy (ECT). I was ready to try anything, but seeing my family cry at the thought of it made me refuse. I decided to stop all medications, relying solely on willpower. It didn't work.

It took years of educating myself about mental health, learning about mindfulness, and changing my perspective to find some semblance of peace. I started practicing controlled breathing, avoided anything with a dark undertone, and focused on living in the present. Volunteering as a mental health supporter online gave me a sense of purpose. Helping others with their issues helped me understand my own better. It was through these interactions that I realized the importance of creating a compassionate society free of stigmatization.

So, why did I write this book? In "Probing Freewill," I discussed how mental health issues limit human autonomy and free will. In "This is not Education," I highlighted the detrimental effects of our educational systems on mental health. This book takes those single chapters and turns it into a holistic, practical, and compassionate guide for individuals struggling with depression and other mental health issues, and for those close to them.

We need to understand that mental health issues are not just about willpower. Just as you wouldn't tell a diabetic to start producing more insulin, you can't tell a depressed person to just be happier. It's a real issue that needs medical attention and societal support. This book is a call to action to make the world a better place—one with better morals, a supportive culture, and a compassionate society.

In these pages, you'll find a blend of personal anecdotes and philosophical reflections. The purpose is to humanize the experience of depression and provide practical advice. I want this book to be a beacon of hope for those struggling, a guide for those trying to understand, and a call for societal change.

Our world is so focused on efficiency and productivity that humanity often gets lost. I remember a colleague who had a therapist's note explaining his mental health struggles. Yet, he was coerced by his employer to be more productive, to just focus and get better. This level of ignorance is harmful. We need to prioritize humanity over progress, community over self-serving greed, and global betterment over national interests.

I hope this book starts a conversation about mental health, educates people on recognizing the signs, and provides strategies for managing depression. But more importantly, I hope it fosters empathy and understanding, breaking down the barriers of stigma and promoting a compassionate approach to mental health.

Let's create a world where mental health is taken seriously, where those struggling feel supported, and where we all work towards a kinder, more understanding society.

I came across the following poem in a long forgotten text. I don't know where it came from or what the book is even called. The original text was in Sanskrit, but here's a rough translation:

"And it all resides inside of you,
If you can go within your spiritual heart,
Your Hridayam,
You will then know; that you are He.

And it is from this place in our heart caves,
Where we are now,
We watch the entire drama; that is our lives,
We watch this illusion,
With Unbearable Compassion."

—

"There is writing happening,
Maybe that's hard for you to understand,
*I am here, but "**I**" am not here,*
*I am writing, but "**I**" am not writing,*

Inside of me, in the heart cave,
Is a mantra going on that reminds me,
Who "I" really am
In this inner place;

'I AM'

And even as I write, where this mantra is going on
I am just watching
With Great Awe and Wonder

PART 1: UNDERSTANDING

DEPRESSION

Let us start our journey with a deep dive into understanding and identifying depression. When I first grappled with my own mental health issues, the lack of clarity and understanding around depression was one of the most daunting hurdles. It's a topic that's often shrouded in misunderstanding and stigma, making it hard for those suffering to find the help they need. This part of the book aims to break down those barriers, offering a comprehensive look at what depression really is, how it affects people differently, and why it's so important to recognize its signs early.

We start by defining depression in its various forms. Depression isn't just about feeling sad occasionally; it's a crippling mental illness that affects millions. It's essential to differentiate between everyday sadness and clinical depression. We'll explore the clinical definitions, the biochemical underpinnings, and the various types of depression; from Major Depressive Disorder to dysthymia. Understanding these distinctions is critical for anyone trying to walk through this arduous journey.

Next, we delve into how depression can cripple daily functioning. It's not just a mental battle; it's a physical one too. Cognitive impairments, emotional and behavioral changes, and physical symptoms all intertwine, creating a web that's hard to untangle. From personal relationships to professional life, the tentacles of depression reach far and wide, affecting everything. Through personal experiences and broader examples, this chapter will shed light on the impacts depression can have on daily life.

To truly understand depression, we need to look at both its biological and psychological roots. Depression is a tentacled illness influenced by genetic, neurochemical, and environmental factors. In chapter 3, we'll explore the role of neurotransmitters, the brain's structure, and the impact of hormones. But biology is only one piece of the puzzle. Psychological theories, like cognitive-behavioral theories and the role of early experiences, also play a significant part in understanding why some people are more susceptible to depression than others.

Finally, we address one of the most critical and heartbreaking aspects of depression: its link to suicide. Understanding the risk factors, warning signs, and the psychological torment that leads to suicidal thoughts is essential for prevention. We'll discuss how to recognize these signs, how to offer support, and what intervention strategies can save lives. Suicide is often the tragic endgame of untreated depression, and by understanding it better, we can work towards preventing these needless losses.

Part 1 is about laying the foundation and understanding that depression is not a personal failing or a sign of weakness; it's a medical illness that requires compassion, knowledge, and a multifaceted approach to treatment and support. Moving through these chapters, I hope to provide you with the insights needed to recognize depression, understand its impacts, and approach it with the empathy and seriousness it deserves. This journey is deeply personal for me. I've walked this path, felt the weight of depression, and grappled with its many faces. Through these pages, I want to share not just the knowledge I've gained, but the hope that comes from 'understanding'.

When we talk about depression, it's vital to distinguish it from the everyday sadness we all experience. Sadness is a normal human emotion, often triggered by specific events like a loss or disappointment. It's a feeling that, while painful, is typically temporary and subsides with time. Depression, on the other hand, is a medically recognized and pervasive mental illness that extends beyond the bounds of typical sadness. It's a relentless shadow that follows you everywhere, sapping joy from activities you once loved and leaving you feeling hopeless and disconnected.

Imagine this: you receive some bad news, like a project at work not going as planned, or perhaps a falling out with a friend. You feel down for a few days, maybe even a week. But eventually, you bounce back. This is normal sadness; a natural response to life's ups and downs. Depression, however, is not just an exaggerated form of this sadness. It's an entirely different beast. In the words of Robert Sapolski,

"If I had to define major depression in one sentence, I would say, it's a biochemical disorder with a genetic component, and early experience influences, where somebody can't appreciate sunsets. And that's what this disease is about… And when you think about it, that is a very sad thing."

Clinical depression, or Major Depressive Disorder (MDD), is characterized by persistent feelings of sadness and hopelessness, lasting for at least two weeks but often extending into months or even years. It's not triggered by a specific event and doesn't simply go away with time. Depression can affect every aspect of your life, from your energy levels and sleep patterns to your ability to think clearly and make decisions. It's an all-encompassing condition that can make even the simplest tasks feel insurmountable.

One of the most insidious aspects of depression is its ability to strip away your ability to feel pleasure; an experience known as ***anhedonia***. This isn't just about feeling sad; it's about losing the ability to enjoy things that once brought you joy, whether it's your favorite hobby, spending time with loved ones, or even basic pleasures like eating or sleeping well. Anhedonia can make you feel like you're living in a gray, joyless world, cut off from any source of happiness.

Depression also comes with a host of physical symptoms. It's not just a mental battle; it's a physical one too. You might feel constantly tired, despite getting enough sleep. You might experience aches and pains that have no clear physical cause. Your appetite can change dramatically; either eating much more or much less than usual. These physical manifestations can make it hard for others to understand that what you're experiencing is a mental health issue, not just a string of bad days or laziness.

The impact of depression extends to your relationships and social life. It can make you withdraw from friends and family, leaving you feeling isolated and misunderstood. The energy required to maintain social connections can feel overwhelming, leading to further isolation and a vicious cycle of loneliness and despair. It's not uncommon for people with depression to feel like a burden to their loved ones, exacerbating feelings of guilt and worthlessness.

In essence, depression is an illness that affects your mind, body, and soul. It's more than just feeling sad or having a rough patch; it's a deeply penetrative condition that requires understanding, compassion, and appropriate treatment. As we walk deeper into this topic, we need to learn about various forms of depression, their symptoms, and how they differ from the normal emotional responses we all experience. Understanding these distinctions is the first step toward breaking the stigma and providing the support needed for those who suffer from this debilitating condition.

Now before we go on to learn about its symptoms, I repeat this because of its imperative, *"depression is often misunderstood and oversimplified. It's not just feeling down for a day or two; it's a persistent and debilitating condition that impacts every aspect of a person's life."* To grasp the full scope of depression, we need to have knowledge of its clinical definition, symptoms, diagnostic criteria, and the various types that exist. To provide a clear understanding of what depression is from a medical standpoint, let us dive a little deeper into it.

Depression manifests in a variety of symptoms that affect not just mood but also physical health, cognition, and behavior. The symptoms can be broadly categorized into emotional, physical, and cognitive symptoms.

Emotional Symptoms:

- **Persistent Sadness or Low Mood:** One of the hallmark symptoms is a prolonged period of sadness or a feeling of emptiness. This isn't just feeling sad after a bad day; it's an enduring sense of despair that doesn't seem to lift.

- **Anhedonia:** This refers to the loss of interest or pleasure in activities that were once enjoyable. It's as if the color has drained from your world, and nothing seems to bring joy or satisfaction anymore.

- **Feelings of Hopelessness and Helplessness:** Those with depression often feel that their situation is hopeless and that there is nothing they can do to change it. This sense of helplessness can be overwhelming and paralyzing.

- **Guilt and Worthlessness:** A pervasive feeling of guilt or worthlessness is common, often out of proportion to the actual situation. People might feel responsible for things beyond their control, or they may believe they are a burden to others.

Physical Symptoms:

- **Changes in Appetite and Weight:** Depression can lead to significant changes in appetite, resulting in weight loss or gain. Some may find food unappealing, while others might overeat as a form of comfort.

- **Sleep Disturbances:** Insomnia or hypersomnia (excessive sleeping) are typical. People might have trouble falling asleep, staying asleep, or waking up early in the morning and being unable to get back to sleep.

- **Fatigue and Low Energy:** Persistent tiredness or a lack of energy that makes even small tasks feel exhausting is another common symptom. This isn't just feeling tired after a long day; it's a debilitatig exhaustion that doesn't improve with rest.

- **Physical Aches and Pains:** Depression can manifest physically, with symptoms like headaches, stomachaches, and muscle pain, which have no apparent physical cause.

Cognitive Symptoms:

- **Difficulty Concentrating:** Depression often affects cognitive functions, making it hard to concentrate, make decisions, or remember things. It can feel like a mental fog has settled over you, making even simple tasks seem insurmountable.

- **Indecisiveness:** Making decisions, even about minor things, can become incredibly challenging. This can lead to procrastination and a sense of being overwhelmed.

- **Suicidal Thoughts:** In severe cases, depression can lead to thoughts of death or suicide. This is one of the most dangerous symptoms and requires immediate attention and intervention.

Here's a table to make it simple:

Category	Symptoms
Emotional	**Persistent Sadness or Low Mood**: Prolonged period of sadness or emptiness.
	Anhedonia: Loss of interest or pleasure in previously enjoyable activities.
	Feelings of Hopelessness and Helplessness: Overwhelming sense of despair.
	Guilt and Worthlessness: Pervasive feelings of guilt or being a burden.
Physical	**Changes in Appetite and Weight**: Significant weight loss or gain.
	Sleep Disturbances: Insomnia or excessive sleeping.
	Fatigue and Low Energy: Persistent tiredness and exhaustion.
	Physical Aches and Pains: Headaches, stomachaches, muscle pain without physical cause.
Cognitive	**Difficulty Concentrating**: Mental fog, trouble focusing, and remembering.
	Indecisiveness: Challenges in making decisions, leading to procrastination.
	Suicidal Thoughts: Thoughts of death or suicide, requiring immediate attention.

DIAGNOSTIC CRITERIA (DSM-5)

The Diagnostic and Statistical Manual of Mental Disorders, Fifth Edition (DSM-5), provides specific criteria for diagnosing *Major Depressive Disorder* (MDD). According to the DSM-5, at least five of the following symptoms must be present during the same two-week period, and at least one of the symptoms should be either depressed mood or loss of interest or pleasure (anhedonia):

1. ☐ Depressed mood most of the day, nearly every day.

2. ☐ Markedly diminished interest or pleasure in all, or almost all, activities most of the day, nearly every day.

3. ☐ Significant weight loss when not dieting, weight gain, or decrease or increase in appetite nearly every day.

4. ☐ Insomnia or hypersomnia nearly every day.

5. ☐ Psychomotor agitation or retardation nearly every day (observable by others, not merely subjective feelings of restlessness or being slowed down).

6. ☐ Fatigue or loss of energy nearly every day.

7. ☐ Feelings of worthlessness or excessive or inappropriate guilt nearly every day.

8. ☐ Diminished ability to think or concentrate, or indecisiveness, nearly every day.

9. ☐ Recurrent thoughts of death, recurrent suicidal ideation without a specific plan, or a suicide attempt or specific plan for committing suicide.

These symptoms must cause significant distress or impairment in social, occupational, or other important areas of functioning. Moreover, the episode must not be attributable to the physiological effects of a substance or another medical condition.

TYPES OF DEPRESSION

Depression is not a one-size-fits-all diagnosis. It comes in various forms, each with its unique features and treatment approaches. I am going to keep this section fairly short and straightforward because the important thing for you, or your loved one, is to have the illness identified, managed, and treated. We are not training professionals here but rather helping raise awareness and break the stigmatization around it. Here are some of the most common types:

1. Major Depressive Disorder (MDD): MDD is characterized by a combination of symptoms that interfere with a person's ability to work, sleep, study, eat, and enjoy once-pleasurable activities. These symptoms must be present for at least two weeks and represent a change from previous functioning. MDD can occur once in a person's lifetime or recur multiple times.

2. Persistent Depressive Disorder (Dysthymia): Dysthymia is a continuous, long-term form of depression. Symptoms are less severe than those of MDD but are chronic, lasting for at least two years. Individuals with dysthymia may experience brief periods of normal mood, but these periods last less than two months. The persistence of symptoms makes this type of depression particularly challenging.

3. Bipolar Disorder: Previously known as manic-depressive illness, bipolar disorder is characterized by mood swings that include depressive episodes and periods of mania or hypomania. During depressive episodes, individuals experience symptoms of MDD. During manic or hypomanic episodes, they may feel euphoric, full of energy, or unusually irritable. These mood swings can affect sleep, energy, activity, judgment, behavior, and the ability to think clearly.

4. Seasonal Affective Disorder (SAD): SAD is a type of depression that occurs at certain times of the year, usually in the winter when daylight hours are shorter. Symptoms include fatigue, depression, hopelessness, and social withdrawal. Light therapy, psychotherapy, and medications are common treatments for SAD.

5. Postpartum Depression: This type of depression occurs after childbirth. It is more severe than the "baby blues," which many new mothers experience. Postpartum depression can make it difficult for new mothers to complete daily care activities for themselves and/or their babies.

6. Premenstrual Dysphoric Disorder (PMDD): PMDD is a severe, sometimes disabling extension of premenstrual syndrome (PMS). It causes extreme mood shifts that can disrupt daily life and damage relationships. Symptoms typically occur in the week before menstruation and improve within a few days after the onset of the menstrual period.

7. Atypical Depression: Atypical depression is characterized by specific features such as increased appetite or weight gain, excessive sleep, a heavy feeling in the arms or legs, and sensitivity to rejection. Unlike other forms of depression, individuals with atypical depression may experience mood improvements in response to positive events.

8. Psychotic Depression: This is a severe form of depression where individuals experience psychosis, such as delusions (false beliefs) or hallucinations (seeing or hearing things that others do not). These symptoms are typically associated with a depressive theme, such as delusions of guilt, poverty, or illness.

Understanding these different types of depression is important for effective diagnosis and treatment. Each type has unique characteristics and may respond differently to various treatments, which highlights the importance of a tailored approach to mental health care. Overall, depression is a complex illness that goes far beyond simple 'blues'. It affects every aspect of a person's life, from their physical health to their cognitive functioning and emotional well-being. We can better recognize and support those who are struggling by committing a little to understand the symptoms, diagnostic criteria, and different types of depression. This knowledge lays the foundation for empathy, effective intervention, healing and, maybe someday, saving someone's life.

Type of Depression	Description
Major Depressive Disorder (MDD)	Symptoms interfere with work, sleep, study, and enjoyment; must be present for at least two weeks.
Persistent Depressive Disorder (Dysthymia)	Chronic, long-term depression; less severe than MDD but lasts for at least two years.
Bipolar Disorder	Mood swings include depressive episodes and periods of mania/hypomania; affects sleep, energy, and behavior.
Seasonal Affective Disorder (SAD)	Depression occurs in winter when daylight hours are shorter; symptoms include fatigue and social withdrawal.
Postpartum Depression	Severe depression after childbirth; more intense than "baby blues," affects daily care activities.
Premenstrual Dysphoric Disorder (PMDD)	Severe mood shifts before menstruation; disrupts daily life and relationships.
Atypical Depression	Features include increased appetite, excessive sleep, heavy feeling in limbs, and sensitivity to rejection.
Psychotic Depression	Severe depression with psychosis, including delusions or hallucinations related to depressive themes.

RISK FACTORS

Understanding the causes and risk factors of depression is like piecing together a huge puzzle. It means examining genetic predispositions, biochemical imbalances, environmental influences, and psychological factors. Each piece offers a glimpse into why depression occurs, but it's actually the interaction between these factors that truly shapes an individual's experience with this condition.

Let's start with genetics, the blueprint of our existence. Research has shown that depression can run in families, suggesting a genetic link. If you have a parent or sibling with depression, you are about two to three times more likely to develop it yourself. This doesn't mean you are destined to be depressed, but it does increase your vulnerability. Imagine genetics as a loaded gun; the trigger, however, is pulled by other factors. Studies have identified several genes that may contribute to the risk of developing depression.

One of the most well-known is the *serotonin transporter gene* (5-HTTLPR). Variations in this gene can affect how serotonin, a neurotransmitter central for mood regulation, is processed in the brain. Those with a particular variation of this gene may be more susceptible to depression, especially when exposed to stressful life events. This gene-environment interaction is a vivid example of how our biology and experiences are intricately linked. Now I understand that this might sound a little too technical and dry to lay ears, but if I had told you the same about a disease, which could be seen with naked eyes, it would have made a lot of sense. This makes it even more important to understand this, because just like you can't see diabetes, but you still don't blame the diabetics for it because you kind of understand that it's due to underlying hormonal disturbances; it's crucial to understand the significance of depression, and **not** to blame the depressed.

Then come other biochemical factors. Our brains are incredibly sophisticated chemical factories, constantly producing and regulating neurotransmitters that affect our mood and behavior. Depression has long been associated with imbalances in these neurotransmitters, particularly serotonin, norepinephrine, and dopamine. These chemicals act as messengers, transmitting signals between nerve cells. When their levels are off-kilter, it can lead to the symptoms of depression. For instance, serotonin, dubbed the "feel-good" neurotransmitter, is a key player in mood regulation, sleep, and appetite. When serotonin levels are low, it can result in feelings of sadness and anxiety. Many antidepressants, like SSRIs (Selective Serotonin Reuptake Inhibitors), work by increasing the availability of serotonin in the brain.

Similarly, norepinephrine, another important neurotransmitter, is involved in the body's response to stress. It helps regulate alertness and energy levels. An imbalance in norepinephrine can lead to fatigue and a lack of interest in daily activities, common symptoms of depression. And finally, dopamine, known for its involvement in the brain's reward system, influences pleasure and motivation. Low levels of dopamine can contribute to anhedonia (the inability to feel pleasure), a hallmark symptom of depression.

Moving on to the external world, the environment we grow up and live in significantly impacts our mental health. Traumatic experiences, such as abuse, neglect, or the loss of a loved one, can trigger depression. These events can leave deep emotional scars, making it difficult for individuals to cope with stress later in life. Similarly, chronic stress, whether from work, relationships, or financial difficulties, is another potent environmental factor. The constant strain can wear down your resilience, making you more susceptible to depression. It's like trying to hold up a heavy weight day after day; eventually, your arms will give out.

Other environmental factors may include a weak social support or socioeconomic structure. For example, having a strong network of friends and family can act as a buffer against depression while isolation and loneliness can exacerbate feelings of sadness and hopelessness. Simultaneously, individuals facing economic hardship are at a higher risk of developing depression as financial stress can lead to a sense of hopelessness and despair, compounding the challenges of daily life.

Our minds are powerful, often in ways we don't fully understand. Psychological factors, such as personality traits and cognitive styles, can influence the likelihood of developing depression. Think about someone you know who always sees the glass as half empty. This isn't just a charming quirk; it can be a precursor to something more serious. Individuals with a pessimistic outlook tend to interpret events in a negative light, expecting the worst outcomes. This cognitive bias not only colors their view of the present but also distorts their expectations of the future, creating an overbearing sense of hopelessness. Low self-esteem works in tandem with this pessimism, leading individuals to believe that they are unworthy or inadequate, no matter their accomplishments. This constant self-criticism can become a relentless inner dialogue that erodes their mental health over time. Our dark mirrors act as the triggers that succumb us further into the darkness.

Cognitive theories of depression emphasize the input of negative thinking patterns. Aaron Beck, a pioneer in cognitive therapy, proposed that depression is rooted in negative cognitive distortions. These distortions include viewing oneself, the world, and the future in an excessively negative light. For instance, a person might think, *"I am worthless,"* *"The world is unfair,"* and *"Things will never get better."* These thoughts can become automatic and habitual, driving the depressive state.

Imagine waking up every day to a mental fog that turns every silver lining into a thundercloud. Cognitive distortions are like faulty mental filters that magnify the negative aspects of any situation while minimizing the positive. This skewed thinking can lead to *"all-or-nothing"* mindsets, where you view things in black and white terms without acknowledging the details. For example, if you make a mistake at work, instead of seeing it as a learning opportunity, you might think, *"I'm a complete failure.*" Over time, these cognitive distortions become ingrained, leading to a disabling sense of despair and inadequacy.

Similarly, ***learned helplessness***, a concept introduced by psychologist Martin Seligman, also offers insight into depression. It occurs when individuals believe they have no control over their circumstances and stop trying to change their situation. This sense of helplessness can be overwhelming and lead to a passive acceptance of negative outcomes, further entrenching depressive symptoms.

Consider a dog repeatedly exposed to an inescapable shock in an experiment. Eventually, even when given the opportunity to escape, the dog no longer tries, having learned that its actions have no effect on the outcome. Humans can experience a similar phenomenon. When faced with repeated failures or uncontrollable stressors, people may develop a sense of helplessness. They begin to believe that their efforts are futile, leading to passivity and resignation. This mindset can be particularly dangerous as it saps the motivation to seek help or make changes, trapping individuals in a cycle of depression. This is no different from how humans control animals by tying them up in their earlier years, instilling in them the traits of conformance and obedience despite their large size and strength in their adulthood.

Another psychological factor that can contribute to depression is perfectionism. On the surface, striving for perfection might seem like a positive trait, but it often masks deep-seated fears of failure and inadequacy. Perfectionists set unrealistically high standards for themselves and are excessively critical when they fall short. This constant pressure can lead to chronic stress and feelings of unworthiness. The fear of failure can be so paralyzing that it prevents individuals from taking risks or pursuing opportunities, reinforcing feelings of stagnation and dissatisfaction. So don't be vary of improving your craft, but the next time you find yourself pursuing perfection, just remember to keep yourself in check.

Rumination or overthinking, the tendency to continuously think about the same negative thoughts, is a common cognitive pattern in depression. It's like being stuck in a mental hamster wheel, where your mind keeps spinning on problems and past mistakes without moving forward. This overthinking can exacerbate depressive symptoms by preventing individuals from finding solutions or gaining perspective. Instead of allowing themselves to process and move past their thoughts, ruminators get trapped in a cycle of negativity that deepens their depression.

Our relationships and social interactions are key components of our mental health. People with depression often experience difficulties in their relationships, which can further exacerbate their symptoms. Poor social skills, difficulty in communicating, and a tendency to withdraw can lead to conflicts and isolation. These interpersonal issues can create a vicious cycle, where depression leads to strained relationships, which in turn deepen the feelings of loneliness and despair.

Early life experiences, such as trauma or neglect, can have a penetrative impact on mental health and the development of depression. Children who grow up in unstable or abusive environments are at a higher risk for developing depression later in life. These early experiences shape their worldview and can lead to persistent feelings of insecurity and mistrust. The psychological scars left by trauma can affect how individuals perceive and respond to stress, making them more vulnerable to depression.

Furthermore, cultural and societal expectations also influence the psychological factors contributing to depression. In cultures that place a high value on achievement and success, individuals may feel immense pressure to meet these standards. Failure to do so can result in feelings of inadequacy and self-blame. Additionally, societal stigma surrounding mental health can prevent individuals from seeking help, further exacerbating their condition. The fear of being judged or misunderstood often leads people to suffer in silence, compounding their depression.

It's important to recognize that these psychological factors don't exist in isolation. They interact with each other and with biological and environmental factors to create a complex web that can lead to depression. For example, a person with a genetic predisposition to depression might also have low self-esteem and a tendency to ruminate on negative thoughts. When faced with a stressful life event, these factors can converge, triggering a depressive episode.

Similarly, it's helpful to examine genetic, biochemical, environmental, and psychological factors individually, depression rarely stems from a single cause. More often, it's the result of an intricate interaction between these elements. For example, just like above, someone with a particular cognitive style might only experience depression when biochemical imbalances are present. Understanding this interplay is imperative. It highlights the importance of a holistic approach to treatment, one that addresses multiple faces of an individual's life. Therapy might focus on changing negative thought patterns, while medication helps to correct biochemical imbalances. Lifestyle changes, such as improving diet and exercise, can provide additional support.

Depression is a tentacled condition with roots in our genes, brain chemistry, environment, and psychological makeup. It's not just about having a bad day or feeling sad; it's a perplexing web of factors that can deeply impact a person's life. We can better comprehend the complexity of depression and approach treatment with the empathy and comprehensiveness it deserves by understanding these causes and risk factors. This knowledge lays the foundation for recognizing, supporting, and effectively treating those affected by this debilitating condition.

Category	Risk Factors
Genetic Factors	**Family History**: Depression can run in families, increasing your risk.
	Serotonin Transporter Gene: Variations may make you more susceptible, especially under stress.
Biochemical Factors	**Neurotransmitter Imbalances**: Low levels of serotonin, norepinephrine, and dopamine can contribute to depression.
	Hormonal Changes: Imbalances affecting mood and behavior.
Environmental Factors	**Traumatic Experiences**: Abuse, neglect, or loss of a loved one can trigger depression.
	Chronic Stress: Persistent stress from work, relationships, or finances increases risk.
	Weak Social Support: Isolation and loneliness exacerbate depression.
	Socioeconomic Status: Financial difficulties heighten the sense of hopelessness.
Psychological Factors	**Negative Cognitive Styles**: Pessimism, low self-esteem, and negative thinking patterns.
	Learned Helplessness: Feeling powerless to change your situation.
	Perfectionism: Unrealistic standards leading to chronic stress and feelings of inadequacy.
	Rumination: Overthinking and dwelling on negative thoughts.
	Interpersonal Issues: Poor social skills and relationship difficulties.
	Early Life Trauma: Unstable or abusive environments during childhood.
	Cultural and Societal Pressures: High achievement expectations and mental health stigma.

Understanding depression involves not only recognizing its symptoms and causes but also distinguishing it from other mood disorders. While **Major Depressive Disorder** (MDD) is a profound and persistent condition, other mood disorders like bipolar disorder, anxiety disorders, and situational depression share some similarities yet remain distinct. Drawing these distinctions is key for accurate diagnosis and effective treatment. We are going to peruse through them, but always remember that this book is to get a general understanding of the illness and how to manage it on a day-to-day basis, it is not a comprehensive academic exploration of the subject. It will help you understand and identify the illness and learn how to manage, but know that just like any other illness, like cancer and so on, the medical intricacies of the illness are too far and wide to be covered in any single book.

Now, let's begin with **bipolar disorder**, formerly known as manic-depressive illness. Bipolar disorder is characterized by significant mood swings that include depressive episodes similar to those seen in MDD, but also periods of mania or hypomania. Imagine your mood as a pendulum. In bipolar disorder, this pendulum swings dramatically from the depths of depressive episodes to the heights of manic phases. During manic episodes, individuals may experience elevated mood, increased energy, decreased need for sleep, and grandiosity. They might engage in risky behaviors, feel euphoric, or become unusually irritable.

Contrast these with the symptoms of MDD, which exhibits profound sadness, lack of interest in activities, fatigue, and feelings of worthlessness. The key difference lies in the presence of these manic or hypomanic episodes, which are absent in MDD. In my experience with MDD, the mood was consistently low, without the high peaks of mania. The unrelenting nature of depression made even simple daily tasks seem Herculean. Bipolar disorder, however, involves navigating both the depths of depression and the peaks of mania, making it a challenging condition to manage.

Secondly, anxiety disorders and depression often coexist, creating a challenging combination. While they share some symptoms, such as irritability and difficulty concentrating, they are distinct in their primary manifestations. Anxiety disorders encompass a range of conditions, including **Generalized Anxiety Disorder** (GAD), **Panic Disorder**, and **Social Anxiety Disorder**. These conditions are characterized by excessive, uncontrollable worry about various aspects of life, even when there is little or no reason to worry. Imagine living in a constant state of alert, where your mind is perpetually racing, heart pounding, and muscles tensed, as if anticipating an imminent threat. This is the essence of an anxiety disorder. In GAD, for example, the worry is omnipresent, affecting multiple areas of life, from work to personal relationships. Panic disorder involves sudden, intense episodes of fear (panic attacks) that can feel like a heart attack.

While MDD is marked by persistent sadness and a lack of interest in life, anxiety disorders revolve around chronic worry and fear. However, the two often overlap. For instance, my MDD included periods of intense anxiety, where the depressive thoughts *triggered* anxious responses. The co-occurrence of depression and anxiety can create a debilitating cycle, where the symptoms of one exacerbate the other.

Next, we have **situational depression**, also known as adjustment disorder with depressed mood,which arises in response to a specific stressful event or situation. Unlike MDD, which can occur without an identifiable trigger, situational depression is directly linked to external circumstances. *Picture this*: you've lost a job, ended a significant relationship, or faced a major life transition. The overwhelming stress and emotional pain from these events can lead to situational depression. Symptoms include sadness, tearfulness, and a feeling of being overwhelmed. These symptoms are similar to those of MDD but are directly tied to the stressful event. The critical difference is the duration and context. Situational depression typically resolves once the individual adapts to the change or the situation improves. It's a temporary response to a life event. MDD, on the other hand, persists for at least two weeks and often much longer, regardless of external circumstances.

In my experience with MDD, there was no singular event that triggered the depressive episodes. It was a persistent cloud, hovering regardless of life's circumstances. Situational depression, while serious, tends to lift as the person adjusts to the new reality or the stressor is removed. It's not uncommon for these disorders to overlap, creating an elaborate clinical picture. For example, a person with bipolar disorder may also experience anxiety disorders. Someone with MDD might have periods of situational depression triggered by life events. This overlap can complicate diagnosis and treatment.

A common misconception is that all mood disturbances are the same or that one can simply *"**snap out of it**."* However, understanding the details of these conditions is vital for appropriate intervention. Each disorder has its unique challenges and requires tailored treatment approaches. However, while MDD, bipolar disorder, anxiety disorders, and situational depression have distinct features, there are commonalities in their treatment. Psychotherapy, particularly Cognitive Behavioral Therapy (CBT), is effective across these conditions. CBT helps individuals recognize and change negative thought patterns and behaviors.

Medication is also a cornerstone of treatment. Antidepressants, such as SSRIs, are commonly used for MDD and anxiety disorders. Mood stabilizers and antipsychotics are essential for managing bipolar disorder. It's essential to work closely with a healthcare provider to find the right medication and dosage. Moreover, lifestyle changes, such as regular exercise, a healthy diet, and adequate sleep, play a significant role in managing these disorders. Mindfulness practices and stress-reduction techniques can also be beneficial.

Living with MDD taught me the importance of understanding and differentiating between these mood disorders. It's not just about labeling the condition but about understanding the unique experiences and challenges each person faces. This knowledge breeds empathy and provides a foundation for effective support and treatment. Remember that navigating mental health is a journey, full of obstacles and misunderstandings. We need to better support those who struggle and advocate for comprehensive mental health care.

DEPRESSION IN DIFFERENT AGE GROUPS

Depression doesn't discriminate. It affects people of all ages, backgrounds, and walks of life, but it doesn't look the same for everyone. Understanding how depression manifests across different demographics; children, adolescents, adults, and the elderly, is necessary for recognizing and addressing it effectively. Each group experiences and expresses depression in unique ways, influenced by their developmental stage, life experiences, and social context.

Depression in Children

Children are not immune to depression, though it can be harder to recognize. Their emotional and psychological frameworks are still developing, making it difficult for them to articulate their feelings. Instead, depression in children often manifests through behavioral and physical symptoms.

Signs and Symptoms:

- **Irritability and Anger:** Unlike adults, who may exhibit sadness or withdrawal, children often show increased irritability, anger, or defiance. They might have frequent temper tantrums or act out in school.

- **Physical Complaints:** Children with depression may frequently complain of physical ailments such as stomach aches or headaches, which don't have a clear medical cause.

- **Changes in Play:** Depression can alter a child's play behavior. They might lose interest in activities they once enjoyed or play out themes of sadness and hopelessness.

- **Academic Decline:** A sudden drop in school performance can be a red flag. Difficulty concentrating and lack of motivation can hinder their academic achievements.

When I was in third grade, I wrote a poem about unrequited love and death. Even at that young age, I felt a pervasive darkness, though I couldn't fully understand or express it. This early manifestation of depressive themes in my writing was a sign that something was amiss, even if it wasn't recognized as such at the time.

Depression in Adolescents

The teenage years are tumultuous, filled with physical, emotional, and social changes. When the hormonal changes in your body are taking place alongside the imbalance caused by depression, the consequent havoc creates a shroud of consistent psychological pain. For adolescents, this depression can blend into the backdrop of typical teenage angst, making it harder to identify. Yet, the stakes are high; untreated depression in adolescence can lead to severe consequences, including academic failure, substance abuse, and even suicide.

Signs and Symptoms:

- **Moodiness and Irritability:** Much like in children, adolescents might show irritability rather than overt sadness. Mood swings are common, but persistent moodiness can signal depression.

- **Social Withdrawal:** Teens might withdraw from friends and family, isolating themselves. They may spend more time alone in their rooms or lose interest in social activities.

- **Risky Behaviors:** Depression can lead to increased risk-taking behaviors, such as substance abuse, reckless driving, or unsafe sexual practices.

- **Academic and Extracurricular Decline:** A drop in grades, missing school, or quitting sports and clubs can be signs of depression. The lack of motivation and energy affects their ability to keep up with their responsibilities.

During my teenage years, I struggled with an existential crisis, feeling like an alien on Earth. This strange sense of not belonging, coupled with social pressures and anxiety, intensified my depressive symptoms. I tried to change my external manifestations to feel different, but nothing worked. It was a clear sign that my depression was more than just teenage angst, but neither me nor anyone around me understood depression, or any mental illnesses for that matter!

Depression in Adults

Adulthood brings its own set of challenges; careers, relationships, parenting, and financial responsibilities. Depression in adults can be particularly insidious, as it often overlaps with these stressors, making it difficult to pinpoint the exact cause. Most adults are often dismissed of having these issues under the emblem of **_"it's normal to feel this way."_** It's only when the illness shows devastating symptoms that we truly realize what has transpired, and by then, like all serious illnesses, the depression has already materialized into an untamed beast.

Signs and Symptoms:

- **Persistent Sadness:** Adults often experience a deep and persistent sadness or emptiness. This is more than just feeling down after a tough day; it's an ongoing emotional pain that doesn't go away.

- **Loss of Interest:** A hallmark of depression is anhedonia—the loss of interest in activities once enjoyed. This can affect hobbies, social interactions, and even sex drive.

- **Physical Symptoms:** Depression in adults often manifests physically, with symptoms like chronic pain, fatigue, and changes in appetite or sleep patterns.

- **Cognitive Difficulties:** Adults with depression might have trouble concentrating, making decisions, or remembering things. This can impact their professional and personal lives significantly.

In my early twenties, I felt isolated and disconnected from the world. My depression affected every decision I made, from my career choices to my personal relationships, casting a long shadow over my life. I remember voicing my frustration to the psychologist that it was such an unfortunate thing that we had to sit in a professional setting, paying someone just to have an open conversation about emotions and feelings because there was no one outside who had the time or the patience to have this conversation with me. The stigma around mental illnesses causes us to hide it from the world, until it often gets out of hand. How unfortunate for us all.

Depression in the Elderly

Depression in the elderly is often overlooked, mistaken for the normal effects of aging. However, it is a serious issue that can significantly impair quality of life and overall health. For seniors, depression can be linked to physical health problems, loss of loved ones, and the transition from active to retired life. It is imperative that we look for these signs and make sure that we do everything that we can, to grab this illness at its roots and intervene with the best of our abilities.

Signs and Symptoms:

- **Physical Complaints:** Older adults often express depression through physical symptoms such as chronic pain, fatigue, and gastrointestinal issues. These symptoms can be mistakenly attributed solely to aging or medical conditions.

- **Cognitive Decline:** Depression can mimic dementia, with symptoms like memory problems, confusion, and slower thinking. This is sometimes referred to as "pseudodementia."

- **Withdrawal and Isolation:** Seniors may withdraw from social activities and family interactions. This isolation can further exacerbate feelings of loneliness and depression.

- **Sleep Disturbances:** Changes in sleep patterns, such as insomnia or excessive sleeping, are common in elderly depression. This can worsen existing health issues and impact daily functioning.

Age Group	Signs and Symptoms
Children	**Irritability and Anger**: Increased irritability, anger, defiance.
	Physical Complaints: Frequent stomachaches or headaches without clear medical cause.
	Changes in Play: Loss of interest in activities, play themes of sadness.
	Academic Decline: Sudden drop in school performance, difficulty concentrating.
Adolescents	**Moodiness and Irritability**: Persistent moodiness, irritability.
	Social Withdrawal: Isolating from friends and family, spending more time alone.
	Risky Behaviors: Substance abuse, reckless driving, unsafe sexual practices.
	Academic and Extracurricular Decline: Drop in grades, missing school, quitting activities.
Adults	**Persistent Sadness**: Deep, ongoing sadness or emptiness.
	Loss of Interest: Anhedonia affecting hobbies, social interactions, sex drive.
	Physical Symptoms: Chronic pain, fatigue, changes in appetite or sleep patterns.
	Cognitive Difficulties: Trouble concentrating, making decisions, remembering things.
Elderly	**Physical Complaints**: Chronic pain, fatigue, gastrointestinal issues.
	Cognitive Decline: Memory problems, confusion, slower thinking (pseudodementia).
	Withdrawal and Isolation: Reducing social activities, family interactions.
	Sleep Disturbances: Insomnia or excessive sleeping, worsening existing health issues.

Recognizing depression in the elderly is very important, as they might be less likely to seek help. Social stigma and generational attitudes towards mental health can prevent older adults from acknowledging their depression and pursuing treatment. Most of the people from the previous generations are unaware of these issues and often dismiss even acknowledging them. It's our responsibility to educate the world about this fundamental aspect of life so the next time we see someone in need, we know how to help them. And in doing so, maybe we leave behind a world, where we equip the coming generations with the gift of community and compassion.

The Importance of Tailored Approaches

Each demographic requires a tailored approach to recognize and treat depression effectively. For children and adolescents, early intervention is key. Educators, parents, and healthcare providers must be vigilant in noticing changes in behavior and mood. Providing a supportive environment where young people feel safe to express their feelings is critical.

For adults, balancing professional responsibilities and personal life is often a significant stressor. Employers and organizations must play a positive part by promoting mental health awareness and providing resources for employees. Therapy and medication can be effective, but lifestyle changes, such as regular exercise, a healthy diet, and stress management techniques, are also essential and must be encouraged.

In the elderly, addressing both physical and mental health is vital. Regular medical check-ups that include mental health screenings can help identify depression early. Encouraging social interactions, whether through family visits, community activities, or technology, can combat isolation. Treatment often involves a combination of therapy, medication, and support from caregivers.

Depression manifests differently across various stages of life, but the impact is universally piercing. Recognizing these differences is the first step in providing the necessary support and treatment. Whether it's a child showing irritability, a teenager withdrawing from friends, an adult struggling with persistent sadness, or an elderly person experiencing chronic pain and cognitive decline, each sign is a call for help. Understanding these unique expressions of depression in different demographics allows us to approach this condition with empathy and precision. It highlights the importance of a comprehensive, tailored approach to mental health that considers the individual's age, life stage, and personal circumstances.

Recognizing depression is the first critical step in addressing this prevalent and debilitating condition. Throughout this chapter, we've explored the clinical definition of depression, distinguishing it from everyday sadness and other mood disorders. We've ventured into the various forms depression can take, from Major Depressive Disorder (MDD) to dysthymia, each with its unique characteristics and impacts on individuals' lives. Understanding these distinctions is imperative for both sufferers and those around them to approach the condition with empathy and precision.

Depression is not just about feeling sad; it's a deep disruption of normal functioning, affecting emotional, physical, and cognitive aspects of life. Persistent sadness, anhedonia, fatigue, cognitive difficulties, and physical symptoms are all part of the complex mosaic that defines depression. These symptoms are not mere inconveniences but massive barriers that can hinder every aspect of a person's life, from their professional achievements to their personal relationships.

Our exploration of the DSM-5 criteria has highlighted the importance of a structured approach to diagnosis. With at least five specific symptoms required for a diagnosis, including a persistent depressed mood or loss of interest in activities, the

DSM-5 provides a framework that helps clinicians identify and treat depression effectively. This diagnostic clarity is essential for ensuring that individuals receive the appropriate care and support they need. Furthermore, understanding the different types of depression emphasizes that there is no one-size-fits-all approach to mental health. Each type requires tailored treatment strategies that address the specific needs of the individual. For instance, while medication might be critical for someone with MDD, a person with situational depression might benefit more from psychotherapy and lifestyle changes.

Recognizing depression early can significantly alter the trajectory of the illness. Early intervention can prevent the condition from worsening, reduce the duration of depressive episodes, and improve overall outcomes. It's important to be vigilant about the signs of depression, whether in oneself or in others. Changes in mood, behavior, and physical health should not be ignored or dismissed as mere phases or personal failings. They are signals that something deeper is going on.

In my own experience, early recognition and intervention would have been key to managing depression but unfortunately, weren't. The sooner we identify and address the signs, the better our chances of finding effective treatment and support. Depression is a formidable adversary, but with awareness, understanding, and a proactive approach, it can be managed.

To wrap up, recognizing the signs of depression early is not just about diagnosis; it's about empathy, support, and a commitment to mental well-being. It's about breaking down the stigma that surrounds mental health issues and creating a compassionate environment where individuals feel safe to seek help. Whether you are experiencing symptoms yourself or noticing them in someone you care about, take action. Reach out, offer support, and seek professional help. We can make a significant difference in the lives of those affected by this challenging condition by doing this.

As we move forward in this book, we will explore the causes and risk factors of depression, the difference between depression and other mood disorders, and how it manifests across different demographics. Each chapter will build on the foundation laid here, deepening our understanding and providing practical strategies for managing and supporting those with depression. Let's continue this journey with open minds and compassionate hearts, ready to learn, understand, and make a difference.

Chapter 2: The Impact of Depression on Daily Life

Depression is a thief. It doesn't just steal joy; it robs you of the ability to function in your daily life. Imagine waking up each morning with an invisible weight pressing down on you, making even the simplest tasks feel insurmountable. This is the daily reality for those living with depression. It seeps into every aspect of life, altering how you think, feel, and act, and it leaves no stone unturned. Depression clouds your mind, making concentration and decision-making difficult. It's like trying to think through a dense fog. Tasks that once seemed routine, like balancing a checkbook or remembering appointments, become Herculean efforts. Your mind can feel sluggish, thoughts muddled, and memory unreliable. This cognitive impairment can affect your professional life, academic performance, and even personal relationships, as keeping track of conversations and commitments becomes increasingly challenging.

Emotionally, depression turns your world gray. It drains you of motivation and energy, making it hard to find pleasure in activities you once enjoyed. You might find yourself withdrawing from social activities, not because you want to, but because the energy it takes to interact with others feels overwhelming. This withdrawal can lead to increased isolation, creating a vicious cycle where you feel lonely and disconnected, yet too exhausted to seek out the connection you crave.

Behaviorally, depression can lead to significant changes. You might find yourself sleeping too much or too little, eating more or less than usual, and neglecting personal hygiene and self-care. These changes aren't just inconvenient; they can lead to serious health problems if left unchecked.

The physical toll of depression is profound. It's not just in your head; it's in your body too. Chronic fatigue, unexplained aches and pains, and gastrointestinal issues are common physical manifestations of depression. Your immune system can become compromised, making you more susceptible to illnesses. The mind-body connection is powerful, and depression can wreak havoc on your physical health just as much as it does on your mental well-being.

Depression doesn't just affect you; it affects those around you. Relationships can become strained as loved ones struggle to understand what you're going through. You might feel guilty for not being able to engage fully with your partner, children, or friends. The irritability and mood swings that often accompany depression can create tension and misunderstandings, leading to conflict and further isolation.

It's a lonely illness. The more you pull away, the harder it becomes for others to reach out, and this disconnection can exacerbate feelings of hopelessness and despair. Building and maintaining healthy relationships while grappling with depression requires significant effort and understanding from both you and those around you.

To truly grasp the impact of depression on daily life, imagine a typical day for someone struggling with this condition. Waking up is a battle in itself, the bed feeling like a safe haven and a prison all at once. Getting ready for work or school is fraught with anxiety and a sense of impending doom. Every interaction, every task is tinged with a sense of futility. By the end of the day, exhaustion sets in, not just from the physical activities but from the constant mental and emotional strain.

Understanding how depression affects daily functioning is imperative for providing effective support and treatment. It's not enough to tell someone to "**snap out of** it" or "**just try harder**." Recognizing the ubiquitous nature of depression allows us to approach it with the empathy and seriousness it deserves. It's about seeing the whole person and understanding the myriad ways depression can impact their life.

As we dive deeper into this chapter, we explore how depression affects cognitive functions, emotional and behavioral patterns, physical health, and relationships. Each section will provide a detailed look at these aspects, offering insights and strategies for managing the daily challenges of living with depression.We can better support those who are struggling and work towards creating a more compassionate and informed society by understanding these impacts.

COGNITIVE EFFECTS

Depression is often considered an emotional illness, but its impact extends far beyond mood. It deeply affects cognitive functions such as memory, concentration, and decision-making. These cognitive deficits can disrupt daily life, making it difficult to perform even the most routine tasks. That's why the illness is considered so pervasive, because it has detrimental effects on every facet of your life.

Memory

Memory problems are a common complaint among those with depression. It's not just about forgetting where you left your keys; it's a major issue that can affect both short-term and long-term memory.

Short-term memory, or working memory, is vital for day-to-day functioning. It allows us to hold and manipulate information temporarily, such as remembering a phone number long enough to dial it or keeping track of ingredients while cooking. Depression can impair this ability, making it challenging to follow conversations, complete tasks, or remember recent events. This can lead to frustration and a sense of incompetence. Imagine trying to read a book but forgetting what happened in the previous paragraph. Each page feels like starting anew, making it impossible to follow the storyline. This is the daily reality for many with depression. Their minds struggle to retain and process new information, leading to a constant feeling of being overwhelmed.

Depression also affects long-term memory, which stores information over extended periods. People with depression often report difficulty recalling past events, especially positive ones. This bias towards negative memories can reinforce feelings of hopelessness and despair. It's as if the brain selectively remembers the bad and forgets the good, further entrenching the depressive state. For example, reflecting on a recent vacation, someone with depression might struggle to recall the joy of the trip, focusing instead on minor inconveniences or moments of anxiety. This selective memory reinforces their negative view of life, perpetuating the cycle of depression.

Concentration

Concentration is another cognitive function significantly impaired by depression. The inability to focus can affect all areas of life, from professional tasks to personal hobbies. Whether in school or at the workplace, concentration is key to productivity and performance. Depression can make it difficult to focus on tasks, leading to errors, missed deadlines, and decreased efficiency. It's not uncommon for individuals with depression to find themselves staring at a computer screen, unable to process the information in front of them. This lack of focus can lead to job insecurity and increased stress, exacerbating the depression. Imagine trying to complete a project but being unable to concentrate long enough to make any progress. The mind wanders, and tasks that should take minutes stretch into hours. This not only affects job performance but also self-esteem and career prospects.

For students, concentration issues can severely impact academic performance. Reading assignments, studying for exams, and participating in class require sustained focus, which depression undermines. As grades slip, anxiety and self-doubt grow, creating a feedback loop that deepens the depressive symptoms. Consider a student preparing for a major exam. Depression makes it hard to concentrate on studying, and during the exam, the mind blanks out, unable to recall studied material. This cycle of poor performance and increasing stress can feel insurmountable.

Even hobbies and personal interests suffer. Activities that once provided joy and relaxation become sources of frustration. Whether it's reading a book, gardening, or engaging in a favorite sport, the inability to concentrate strips these activities of their pleasure. For instance, a painter might find it impossible to focus on their work, their mind wandering and their brushstrokes lacking the precision and creativity they once had. This can lead to abandoning hobbies altogether, further isolating the individual.

Decision-Making

Decision-making is a mixture of many cognitive processes that depression severely disrupts. The condition often leads to indecisiveness, procrastination, and poor judgment. Depression can make even simple decisions feel monumental. Choosing what to wear, what to eat, or which route to take can become overwhelming. This indecisiveness stems from a lack of confidence in one's judgment and a fear of making the wrong choice. Imagine standing in the grocery store aisle, unable to decide between two brands of cereal. What should be a quick decision stretches into an agonizing deliberation, leaving you feeling frustrated and defeated. This unescapable indecisiveness affects all areas of life, from mundane daily choices to significant life decisions.

We are all accustomed to the demons of procrastination. But it is less common to know that procrastination is often linked to depression. The overwhelming sense of fatigue and lack of motivation can make it difficult to start or complete tasks. This delay in decision-making can lead to missed opportunities and increased stress, creating a vicious cycle that reinforces the depressive symptoms. A form of 'negative feedback loop' where each negative feedback results in another negative action. For example, you might delay making a doctor's appointment, knowing it's important but feeling too overwhelmed to take the step. As days turn into weeks, the unmade decision adds to your stress and anxiety.

Depression can further impair judgment, leading to decisions that might seem irrational to others. This poor judgment is often influenced by the negative cognitive distortions common in depression. You might underestimate your abilities, overestimate risks, or focus on short-term relief at the expense of long-term consequences. Consider someone with depression deciding to quit their job impulsively, convinced they can't handle the work despite no evidence of poor performance. This decision, driven by distorted thinking, can lead to significant financial and personal repercussions.

The cognitive effects of depression; impairments in memory, concentration, and decision-making are vast and far-reaching. They impact every aspect of daily life, from professional responsibilities to personal relationships and hobbies. Recognizing these cognitive deficits is integral for understanding the full scope of depression's impact and for developing effective coping strategies and treatments. Depression isn't just an emotional struggle; it's a cognitive battle; a mind at war with itself. We can better support those living with depression and help them reclaim their cognitive functions and quality of life by acknowledging and addressing these cognitive effects. As we move forward in this chapter, we must explore how depression affects emotional and behavioral patterns, physical health, and social relationships.

Cognitive Effect	Description
Memory	**Short-term Memory Issues**: Difficulty remembering recent events and holding information.
	Long-term Memory Issues: Struggling to recall past events, especially positive ones.
Concentration	**Impaired Focus**: Trouble concentrating on tasks, leading to errors and decreased efficiency.
	Academic Performance: Difficulty in studying and participating in class.
	Hobbies and Interests: Loss of enjoyment in activities due to lack of focus.
Decision-Making	**Indecisiveness**: Difficulty making even simple decisions, leading to frustration.
	Procrastination: Delaying tasks due to fatigue and lack of motivation.
	Poor Judgment: Making irrational decisions influenced by negative thinking patterns.

EMOTIONAL AND BEHAVIORAL CHANGES

Depression isn't just a series of gloomy thoughts or a constant feeling of sadness; it's an overshadowing shift in how a person experiences and interacts with the world. It alters emotional responses and behaviors, creating patterns that can be hard to break. These changes affect not only the individual but also those around them, often leading to a cycle of misunderstanding and isolation. I remember spending my days in dark rooms in my house and dark places in my head. It's an isolation and darkness that brings more isolation and darkness.

Emotional Changes

While sadness is the most commonly recognized symptom of depression, irritability and mood swings are also dominant, especially in men and adolescents. Depression can manifest as frustration, anger, and irritability. Minor annoyances or inconveniences that would typically be shrugged off can trigger intense emotional reactions. Imagine waking up and immediately feeling on edge. Every little thing; a misplaced key, a slow driver, an offhand comment, sets off a wave of frustration. This irritability isn't just about being in a bad mood; it's a fundamental shift in how one perceives and reacts to the world. It's like having a short fuse, where even the smallest spark can lead to an explosion of anger or frustration.

Further, depression often brings an overwhelming sense of worthlessness and guilt. These emotions aren't tied to specific actions or events; rather, they are toxicating feelings that can dominate a person's inner dialogue. Individuals might constantly berate themselves, feeling as if they are a burden to others, or undeserving of happiness or success. Consider someone who consistently performs well at work yet feels they're failing at their job. Every small mistake or oversight becomes a reflection of their perceived incompetence. This internalized guilt and worthlessness can erode self-esteem, making it difficult to see any positives in oneself.

Depression can also lead to emotional numbness, where individuals feel disconnected from their emotions and the world around them. This numbness can be particularly distressing because it strips away the ability to feel joy, love, or even sadness. It's a void where emotions once existed, leaving a sense of emptiness. Imagine going through the motions of daily life without feeling anything. You watch a comedy, but don't laugh. You hear bad news, but don't cry. This emotional flatness makes it hard to engage with life, creating a sense of detachment from everything and everyone. The colors fade away and, just like that, it's all gray.

Behavioral Changes

One of the most noticeable behavioral changes in depression is social withdrawal. People with depression often isolate themselves, avoiding friends, family, and social activities. This withdrawal isn't about wanting to be alone; it's about feeling unable to connect or fearing that their presence is a burden to others. Picture someone who used to be the life of the party, now consistently declining invitations, not returning calls, and avoiding gatherings. This isolation can deepen the feelings of loneliness and despair, creating a vicious cycle where the less they engage, the harder it becomes to reach out. One often feels like the act of living itself becomes a burden.

Depression saps the desire to do things that once brought pleasure. This loss of interest, "anhedonia," affects hobbies, work, and even daily routines. Activities that were once eagerly anticipated now feel like burdens. Imagine a passionate painter who suddenly stops picking up their brush, or an avid reader who finds no joy in books. This lack of interest can extend to self-care tasks like showering or eating, further deteriorating one's physical and mental health. If you're someone who knows a depressed person, just sit for a moment and contemplate just how debilitating and crippling all of this must feel.

On another front, depression disrupts sleep, causing either insomnia or hypersomnia. Insomnia is where people struggle to sleep, lying awake for hours, their minds racing with negative thoughts. On the other hand, excessive sleep, or hypersomnia, is used as an escape from the painful realities of their waking life. Consider the exhaustion that comes with insomnia, where every day feels like a foggy, uphill battle due to lack of rest. Conversely, imagine the lethargy of oversleeping, waking up groggy and unrefreshed, still feeling the weight of the previous night's despair. Just because one's sleeping excessively does not mean, at all, that they're resting!

Furthermore, depression can lead to significant changes in appetite, resulting in weight loss or gain. Some individuals might lose their appetite entirely, finding food unappealing or feeling too anxious to eat. Others might turn to food for comfort, leading to overeating. For instance, someone might find that they can't stomach even their favorite meals, losing weight as a result. Alternatively, they might find themselves compulsively snacking, gaining weight despite a lack of genuine hunger. *"I eat because it's comforting and distracting!"* These changes can further impact self-esteem and physical health.

In some cases, depression can lead to increased risk-taking behaviors. This might include substance abuse, reckless driving, or impulsive decisions. These behaviors can be a misguided attempt to cope with the overwhelming emotions or to feel something in the midst of numbness. Imagine someone turning to alcohol or drugs to numb their pain, or engaging in dangerous activities just to break the monotony of their emotional flatness. These behaviors often create additional problems, compounding the difficulties they already face.Depression can make it difficult to manage daily responsibilities, from work to household chores. Tasks pile up, bills go unpaid, and work performance suffers. This neglect can lead to significant consequences, exacerbating feelings of failure and hopelessness. Think about the stress of seeing a sink full of dirty dishes or a growing stack of unopened mail. The energy required to tackle these tasks feels insurmountable, leading to further neglect and a deeper sense of being overwhelmed.

The emotional and behavioral changes were some of the most challenging aspects to navigate in my own journey. The irritability and mood swings made interactions with loved ones strained. Social withdrawal led to loneliness, even when surrounded by people. The loss of interest in activities I once loved made life feel hollow and meaningless. Understanding these changes and recognizing them as symptoms of depression, rather than personal failings, is integral. It allows for a compassionate approach to treatment and support, acknowledging the devastating impact depression has on every aspect of life. Depression's emotional and behavioral changes create a ripple effect, impacting not just the individual but everyone around them. Recognizing these changes is vital for early intervention and effective treatment. It's about understanding that these shifts in mood and behavior are part of the illness, not a reflection of the person's character. As we continue to explore the impact of depression on daily life, we will understand how it affects physical health and social relationships. Each section will provide further insights into the nature of this condition, painting a comprehensive picture of what it means to live with depression.

Category	Changes
Emotional Changes	**Irritability and Mood Swings**: Increased frustration and anger, even at minor annoyances.
	Worthlessness and Guilt: Persistent feelings of being a burden and undeserving of happiness.
	Emotional Numbness: Disconnection from emotions, resulting in a lack of joy, love, or even sadness.
Behavioral Changes	**Social Withdrawal**: Avoiding friends, family, and social activities, leading to isolation.
	Loss of Interest (Anhedonia): No longer finding pleasure in hobbies, work, or daily routines.
	Sleep Disruptions: Insomnia or hypersomnia, affecting rest and daily functioning.
	Appetite Changes: Significant weight loss or gain due to changes in eating habits.
	Risk-Taking Behaviors: Increased likelihood of substance abuse, reckless driving, or impulsive actions.
	Neglect of Responsibilities: Difficulty managing daily tasks, leading to further stress and overwhelm.

Depression doesn't only affect the mind; it takes a heavy toll on the body. The physical symptoms of depression are often as debilitating as the emotional and cognitive ones. These symptoms can range from a weakened immune system to chronic pain and loss of libido, each compounding the struggle of daily life. The immune system is often compromised in depression, making you more susceptible to illnesses. The connection between mental health and immune function is a complex interplay of hormones and biochemical responses.

When you're depressed, your body is often in a constant state of stress. This chronic stress leads to the release of stress hormones like cortisol. While short bursts of cortisol can help your body handle immediate threats, prolonged exposure weakens the immune system. It's like running your car engine at full throttle all the time; eventually, something's going to give. Imagine waking up with a cold every other week, or feeling perpetually rundown. These are not just coincidences but manifestations of your body's compromised ability to fend off everyday germs and viruses. I remember periods in my life when I seemed to catch every bug that came around, my body unable to keep up with the demands placed on it by both external pathogens and internal turmoil. You say to yourself, "Why is it always me?!" Well, now you know, it's because you're afflicted with an illness. However, remember the diagnostic criteria so you don't always confuse inner turmoil with depression.

Depression is also linked to increased levels of inflammation. Studies have shown that people with depression often have higher levels of inflammatory markers in their blood. Inflammation is the body's response to injury or infection, but when it becomes chronic, it can lead to various health problems. For instance, you might experience joint pain or frequent headaches. This is not just your body reacting to physical stressors but also to the internal stress of depression. These aches and pains can make it even harder to find the motivation to engage in healthy behaviors, creating a vicious cycle of declining physical health.

Similarly, chronic pain is another common physical symptom of depression. It's not unusual for people with depression to report unexplained aches and pains, which can significantly affect their quality of life. Many people with depression experience musculoskeletal pain, such as back pain, neck pain, or general muscle aches. This pain isn't always attributable to physical activity or injury but is instead a manifestation of the body's overall stress response. Think about waking up every day with a sore back or aching muscles. Even if you haven't done anything strenuous, your body feels like it's been through a marathon. All of this regardless of the amount of sleep or rest you seemingly get. This kind of chronic pain can make it difficult to maintain regular exercise routines or even perform daily tasks, further contributing to a sedentary lifestyle and the physical decline associated with it.

Additionally, headaches and migraines are also common with depression. The constant tension and stress can lead to frequent headaches, which can be debilitating. Imagine trying to get through a workday with a throbbing headache that just won't go away. It's not just a minor inconvenience but a significant barrier to productivity and well-being. I remember my migraines, and I wouldn't ever wish them on anyone. They were crippling. The shooting pain was so bad that I had to take narcotic painkillers to even get some semblance of pain relief.

Moreover, depression can significantly impact sexual health, leading to a loss of libido or interest in sexual activities. This symptom is often overlooked but can have damaging effects on personal relationships and self-esteem. Depression can cause hormonal imbalances that affect sex drive. The same stress hormones that weaken the immune system and cause chronic pain can also interfere with the hormones responsible for sexual desire and function. For instance, elevated levels of cortisol can reduce the production of sex hormones like testosterone and estrogen. This hormonal imbalance can lead to a decreased interest in sex, making it difficult to maintain intimate relationships. It's not just about the physical act but the emotional connection that can suffer as well as you start feeling distant and uninterested in your partner or vice versa.

Many medications prescribed for depression, such as selective serotonin reuptake inhibitors (SSRIs), can also have side effects that reduce libido. This creates a challenging situation where the treatment for depression exacerbates one of its symptoms. Imagine feeling emotionally disconnected from your partner, and on top of that, experiencing a physical disinterest in intimacy. This can lead to feelings of guilt, frustration, and further isolation, adding another layer to the already devastating emotional turmoil of depression.

Understanding the physical symptoms of depression is important because they are often intertwined with emotional and cognitive symptoms and are much easily identifiable. These physical manifestations are not just side effects but integral parts of the depressive experience. The chronic fatigue, pain, and weakened immune system can make everyday activities feel like climbing a mountain. Tasks that were once simple become herculean, contributing to a sense of failure and hopelessness. Consider the effort it takes just to get out of bed in the morning when your body feels like it's weighed down by lead. Each step, each movement requires more energy than you have, making it hard to keep up with daily responsibilities. This physical exhaustion feeds back into the emotional and cognitive aspects of depression, creating a cycle that is difficult to break.

Depression's physical symptoms are as real and impactful as its emotional and cognitive ones. They can add an immeasurable burden on life. These symptoms are not isolated but stretch into our social lives, which is why as we continue to explore the impact of depression on daily life, we will now look at how it affects relationships and social interactions. Each aspect of this condition just weaves into the next, creating a comprehensive picture of the impact depression has on those who live with it.

Physical Effect	Description
Weakened Immune System	**Increased Illness**: More susceptible to colds and infections due to chronic stress and hormonal imbalances.
Chronic Pain	**Musculoskeletal Pain**: Unexplained aches, such as back pain and muscle soreness, impacting daily life.
	Headaches and Migraines: Frequent, debilitating headaches caused by constant tension and stress.
Inflammation	**Joint Pain**: Higher levels of inflammation leading to joint pain and other inflammatory issues.
Fatigue	**Chronic Exhaustion**: Persistent tiredness despite rest, making everyday activities feel overwhelming.
Sleep Disturbances	**Insomnia or Hypersomnia**: Difficulty sleeping or excessive sleeping, affecting overall health and daily functioning.
Appetite Changes	**Weight Loss or Gain**: Significant changes in eating habits, leading to weight fluctuations.
Sexual Health	**Loss of Libido**: Reduced interest in sexual activities due to hormonal imbalances and stress.
	Medication Side Effects: Certain antidepressants can decrease libido, complicating treatment.

As mentioned above, depression casts a long shadow over personal and professional relationships, affecting not only those who suffer from it but also the people around them. It disrupts communication, creates misunderstanding, and can lead to isolation, making it a significant barrier to maintaining healthy relationships and a fulfilling social life.

Personal Relationships

A lot of this happens because one of the first casualties of depression is communication. When you're depressed, expressing yourself can feel like an insurmountable task. Words don't come easily, and when they do, they often don't convey the depth of what you're experiencing. Imagine trying to explain to your partner why you can't get out of bed, why you don't have the energy to engage in a simple conversation, or why their attempts to cheer you up only make you feel worse. It's like speaking a different language, one that's difficult for them to understand. This breakdown in communication can lead to frustration on both sides. Your loved ones might feel helpless, unable to comprehend or alleviate your pain, while you might feel misunderstood and isolated.

Simultaneously it leads to emotional withdrawal, where you pull back from close relationships to avoid burdening others with your struggles. The withdrawal is not a reflection of your feelings towards them but rather a coping mechanism to deal with your own overwhelming emotions. You want to get away from everything. Think of a time when you've felt the need to retreat into yourself, to find solace in solitude because the thought of interacting with others feels too daunting. This self-imposed isolation can create a rift between you and your loved ones, who might interpret your withdrawal as disinterest or rejection. The more you pull away, the more difficult it becomes for them to reach out, perpetuating a cycle of loneliness and misunderstanding.

The loss of libido and emotional numbness discussed earlier severely impact physical and emotional intimacy in relationships. When you're depressed, it's hard to feel connected to your partner, both physically and emotionally. Consider the struggle of maintaining a romantic relationship when you feel disconnected from your own emotions. The effort required to engage in intimate moments feels impossible, and the lack of sexual desire can create tension and misunderstanding. Your partner might feel rejected or inadequate, not realizing that these changes are symptoms of your depression and not a reflection of your feelings towards them.

As could be expected, this also intrudes family dynamics, particularly affecting the parent-child relationship. As a parent, your depression can make it hard to provide the emotional support and engagement your children need. The energy required to care for a child, to be present and attentive, can feel overwhelming. Imagine trying to keep up with the demands of parenting when every day feels like an uphill battle. The guilt of not being able to be the parent you want to be, coupled with the frustration of your children not understanding your struggles, can create significant stress and strain within the family. Your children might become confused or anxious, sensing that something is wrong but not fully understanding what it is.

In contrast, it can also *shift* family dynamics. Spouses or partners might take on additional responsibilities, both emotionally and practically, to compensate for your inability to function at full capacity. This shift can lead to resentment and burnout, further complicating the relationship dynamics. If your partner has to pick up the slack at home, manage household chores, finances, and childcare, the added burden will take a toll on their own well-being even if they do so willingly. The imbalance can lead to feelings of resentment, frustration, and exhaustion, which can make the relationship feel like going through a sieve.

Social Relationships

Social withdrawal is a hallmark of depression, leading to a diminished social life and strained friendships. The energy required to maintain social connections can feel overwhelming, leading you to avoid social gatherings and interactions. A once vibrant social life will now be reduced to occasional texts and rare outings. Friends might not understand why you've become distant, interpreting your absence as disinterest or neglect. The more you withdraw, the harder it becomes to engage and re-engage, leading to a sense of isolation and loneliness.

As a cherry on top, depression is often misunderstood, and the stigma associated with mental illness further complicates social relationships. Friends might offer well-meaning but unhelpful advice, such as "***just cheer up***" or "***try to be more positive***," not realizing the depth of your struggle. Think about the frustration of trying to explain your condition to someone who has never experienced it. Their inability to understand can create an invisible wall, making you feel even more isolated. The stigma surrounding depression can also lead to reluctance in sharing your struggles, fearing judgment or rejection.

In the workplace, the cognitive and emotional symptoms of depression, such as difficulty concentrating, low energy, and irritability, can affect your performance and interactions with colleagues. Imagine struggling to keep up with your workload, missing deadlines, or making mistakes because you can't focus. These issues can lead to conflicts with colleagues and supervisors, who might not understand the underlying cause of your performance issues. The stress of trying to hide your symptoms or explain your situation can further exacerbate your condition.

The impact of depression on your professional life can also affect your career trajectory. Missed opportunities for promotions, decreased productivity, and frequent absences can hinder career advancement and job security. Consider the anxiety of knowing that your job performance is suffering but feeling powerless to change it. The fear of losing your job or being passed over for opportunities can add to your stress and depression, creating a cycle that's hard to break.

The Ripple Effect

The impact of depression on relationships and social life creates a ripple effect, extending beyond the individual to affect everyone around them. The strain on personal, familial, and professional relationships can lead to increased isolation, misunderstandings, and conflicts, making it even harder to cope with depression. It's important for loved ones, friends, and colleagues to be aware of the ways depression can affect relationships and to approach the situation with empathy and patience.

Depression's impact strains communication, stirs emotional withdrawal, and can lead to significant changes in family dynamics, friendships, and professional interactions. Understanding these effects is imperative for creating a supportive environment for those struggling with depression.We can develop a more compassionate and informed approach to mental health if we recognize the persistent nature of depression and its effects on relationships.

Reflecting on the universal nature of depression and its comprehensive impact is essential to understanding the true extent of this debilitating condition. Throughout this chapter, we've explored how depression infiltrates various aspects of daily life, from cognitive functions to emotional well-being, physical health, and relationships. Each aspect reveals the subtle ways depression can undermine the essence of daily living, creating ripples that extend far beyond the individual.

Depression is not just a mood disorder; it is a thief that steals one's cognitive clarity, emotional stability, physical health, and social connections. It clouds the mind, making memory unreliable and concentration nearly impossible. Decision-making becomes a daunting task, filled with indecision and procrastination. The cognitive impairments brought on by depression disrupt daily functioning, impacting professional performance and personal interactions. Emotionally, it drains the color from life. It induces a state of persistent sadness, irritability, and emotional numbness. The constant struggle with worthlessness and guilt can erode self-esteem, making it difficult to see any positives in oneself. The emotional withdrawal that often accompanies depression leads to increased isolation, exacerbating feelings of loneliness and disconnection. These emotional and behavioral changes create a cycle of misunderstanding and tension, affecting not only the individual but also those around them.

Physically, depression takes a significant toll on the body. The weakened immune system, chronic pain, and loss of libido are tangible manifestations of the illness. These physical symptoms are integral parts of the depressive experience, adding an additional burden and making everyday activities feel almost impossible. The chronic fatigue, unexplained aches, and compromised immune system all contribute to the overall decline in physical health, creating a cycle of deterioration. Socially, the inability to express oneself and the tendency to withdraw from interactions creates a wall between the individual and their loved ones. This exacerbates the stigma associated with mental illness, leads to further misunderstandings and isolation.

Recognizing the pervasive nature of depression allows us to approach it with the empathy and seriousness it deserves. It's about seeing the whole person and understanding the many ways depression can impact their life. This understanding is needed for providing effective support and treatment. It's not enough to tell someone to "snap out of it" or "just try harder." Instead, we need to acknowledge the web of factors that contribute to the depressive experience.

Depression is a multifaceted condition that affects every aspect of daily life. It's a battle that is fought not just in the mind but also in the body and in the interactions with the world. As we move deeper into the subsequent chapters, we will understand the foundations of depression and uncover strategies to manage the challenges of living with depression and pave the way towards recovery and resilience.

Depression is a complicated condition, not just a product of external circumstances or internal thoughts, but a continuous interaction between biological and psychological factors that can ensnare even the most resilient individuals. Now before I move on further with this chapter, I must say that it gets a little technical at times because, after all, it is a complicated thing to learn about. So if you start feeling overwhelmed at any point, just skip right over, and you can check back on it whenever you feel comfortable.

Now, when I first began grappling with depression, I often wondered, "Why me?" The answer is neither simple nor singular. Depression's roots are buried deep into our biology, involving neurotransmitters and brain structures, while also branching out into the psychological, influenced by our thoughts, beliefs, and past experiences. This dual nature of depression means that it can strike anyone, regardless of their external circumstances, exhibiting the need for a comprehensive approach to understanding and treating this condition.

On a biological level, depression is often linked to imbalances in neurotransmitters, the chemicals that facilitate communication between nerve cells in the brain. Neurotransmitters like serotonin, dopamine, and norepinephrine play central roles in regulating mood, sleep, and appetite. An imbalance in these chemicals can lead to the symptoms commonly associated with depression, such as persistent sadness, fatigue, and loss of interest in activities. But it's not just about chemicals; brain structure and function are also altered in depression. Areas like the hippocampus, amygdala, and prefrontal cortex show changes in size and activity levels, further contributing to the emotional and cognitive symptoms of depression.

However, focusing solely on the biological aspects would be like reading only half the story. The psychological components of depression are equally significant. Cognitive theories, for instance, emphasize the role of negative thinking patterns and cognitive distortions. These are not just fleeting thoughts but deeply ingrained ways of interpreting the world that can trap individuals in a cycle of negativity. Think of it as wearing glasses that tint everything around you in shades of gray, making it hard to see any brightness or hope.

Moreover, our past experiences, particularly traumatic ones, can leave lasting imprints on our psyche, making us more vulnerable to depression. Trauma can alter our brain chemistry and shape our cognitive patterns, creating a fertile ground for depression to take root. This aspect underscores the importance of addressing both the mind and body when considering treatment options. The psychological impact of trauma is a poignant reminder of how our experiences shape us. In "*The Body Keeps the Score*," Bessel van der Kolk discusses how trauma is stored in our bodies and minds, influencing our mental health long after the traumatic events have passed. This insight is indispensable for understanding why some individuals develop depression and others do not, even when faced with similar life circumstances.

Furthermore, the field of depression research is continually evolving, with new insights shedding light on this complex condition. Genetic studies have started to unravel the hereditary aspects of depression, while innovative therapies, such as transcranial magnetic stimulation (TMS) and ketamine infusions, offer new hope for treatment-resistant depression. These advancements portray the importance of staying informed about the latest research, as they pave the way for more effective and personalized treatment options.

In my own journey, understanding the biological and psychological aspects of depression has been enlightening and empowering. It has helped me realize that my struggle is not a sign of weakness or personal failure but a condition rooted in deep and turbulent causes. This knowledge has guided me towards a more compassionate view of myself and others facing similar battles.

This chapter will explore the neurobiological foundations of depression, examining various psychological theories and considering the impact of trauma. We will also look at the latest research findings that are reshaping our understanding of this condition. Through this exploration, we aim to elucidate the interaction between biology and psychology in depression, to paint a detailed picture that informs more effective and empathetic approaches to treatment and support.

NEUROBIOLOGY

Depression, as I've come to understand through personal experience and extensive research, is deeply rooted in both our biology and psychology. It's a condition that doesn't just affect our thoughts and emotions, but also physically alters our brain's structure and function. Let's look into the neurobiological foundations of depression, focusing on neurotransmitters, brain structure changes, and the hypothalamic-pituitary-adrenal (HPA) axis.

The Role of Neurotransmitters

When I first learned about the biological basis of depression, the concept of neurotransmitters was enlightening. These chemical messengers facilitate communication between neurons in our brain, and any imbalance can significantly impact mood and behavior.

1. **Serotonin:** Often dubbed the "feel-good" neurotransmitter, serotonin is a decisive player for

regulating mood, appetite, and sleep. When serotonin levels are low, it can lead to feelings of sadness and anxiety. Many antidepressants, SSRIs, work by increasing serotonin levels in the brain, alleviating depressive symptoms.

2. **Dopamine:** This neurotransmitter is associated with the brain's reward system and is integral to experiencing pleasure and motivation. In depression, dopamine levels are often diminished, leading to anhedonia, the inability to feel pleasure in normally enjoyable activities. I vividly recall moments when activities that once brought me joy felt meaningless, a clear sign of dopamine imbalance.

3. **Norepinephrine:** This neurotransmitter affects alertness and energy levels. An imbalance can result in fatigue and a lack of interest in daily activities, common symptoms in depressive episodes. I came to realize much later in life that the fluctuating energy levels oscillating between extreme fatigue and the anxiety I experienced indicated norepinephrine's role in my depression.

Brain Structure Changes

The physical alterations in brain structure provide another layer of understanding. Depression is not just a state of mind but also a state of the brain.

1. **Hippocampus:** This region, essential for memory and learning, often shows reduced volume in individuals with depression. Chronic stress, a significant factor in depression, leads to the release of cortisol, which can damage neurons in the hippocampus. I found it fascinating and somewhat alarming to learn that my struggles with memory and concentration were not just

in my head but reflected real changes in our brain structure.

2. **Amygdala:** The amygdala, which processes emotions such as fear and pleasure, tends to be hyperactive in those with depression. This overactivity correlates with the heightened emotional responses and negative biases typical of depression. I could see this clearly in my own exaggerated reactions to stress and conflict, feeling everything more intensely than those around me.

3. **Prefrontal Cortex:** Responsible for decision-making, planning, and social behavior, the prefrontal cortex often shows decreased activity in depressed individuals. This reduction can lead to impaired judgment, decision-making difficulties, and social withdrawal. The foggy thinking and difficulty in making decisions that plagued me during depressive episodes were tied to these functional changes.

The Hypothalamic-Pituitary-Adrenal (HPA) Axis

The HPA axis is a complex system that controls our response to stress. Dysregulation of this axis is a hallmark of depression.

1. **Hypothalamus:** This brain region links the nervous system to the endocrine system via the pituitary gland. In depression, the hypothalamus can become overactive, leading to excessive production of corticotropin-releasing hormone (CRH), which in turn stimulates the pituitary gland.

2. **Pituitary Gland:** In response to CRH, the pituitary gland releases adrenocorticotropic hormone (ACTH). ACTH travels through the bloodstream to the adrenal glands, prompting them to release cortisol. During my

bouts of depression, I often felt like my body was in a constant state of fight-or-flight, a direct result of this cascade of hormonal activity.

3. **Adrenal Glands:** These glands produce cortisol, the stress hormone. While cortisol is essential for dealing with short-term stress, chronic elevation due to HPA axis dysregulation can lead to various health problems, including immune suppression, increased abdominal fat, and even further damage to brain regions like the hippocampus. Understanding this process helped me make sense of the physical symptoms I experienced, like chronic fatigue and susceptibility to illnesses.

The interplay between neurotransmitter imbalances, structural brain changes, and HPA axis dysregulation creates a feedback loop that exacerbates depression. The chronic stress I endured not only affected my mood but also altered my brain's chemistry and structure, perpetuating the cycle of depression.

Addressing depression needs to be approached from multiple fronts. Medications can help balance neurotransmitters, but therapy is equally important to address the psychological aspects and help break negative thinking patterns. Additionally, lifestyle changes such as regular exercise, adequate sleep, and stress management techniques can support both brain health and emotional well-being.

In my journey, understanding the neurobiological aspects of depression has given me previously non-understood tools to deal with depression. It demystified the condition, showing me that my experiences were not merely personal failings but the result of so many biological processes. This knowledge has not only informed my treatment choices but also resurrected a sense of compassion for myself during the most challenging times.

As we continue exploring the biology and psychology of depression, it will become clear that a holistic approach; one that integrates biological, psychological, and social dimensions, is essential for effective treatment and lasting recovery. This understanding is imperative for anyone dealing with depression, either personally or in supporting a loved one.

Psychological Theories

When I first started looking into the reasons behind my depression, I realized that it wasn't just a chemical imbalance in my brain. The psychological theories surrounding depression provided a more comprehensive understanding of my struggles. These theories highlighted how our thoughts, behaviors, and past experiences all play major roles in the development and persistence of depression. Let's explore some of the key psychological theories: cognitive-behavioral theory, learned helplessness, and psychoanalytic perspectives.

Cognitive-Behavioral Theory

The cognitive-behavioral theory, pioneered by Aaron Beck in the 1960s, is one of the most influential models in understanding and treating depression. This theory posits that our thoughts, feelings, and behaviors are interconnected, and that negative thought patterns can lead to and perpetuate depressive symptoms.

Negative Cognitive Triad: Beck identified the "*negative cognitive triad*," which consists of negative views about oneself, the world, and the future. This triad creates a vicious cycle that reinforces depression. For instance, I often found myself thinking, "I am worthless," "The world is a harsh place," and "Things will never get better." These thoughts were not just fleeting; they became automatic and deeply ingrained, coloring every aspect of my perception.

Cognitive Distortions: Cognitive distortions are irrational thought patterns that can contribute to depression. These include:

- **All-or-Nothing Thinking:** Seeing things in black and white terms. If something isn't perfect, it's a total failure. For example, if I didn't complete a task perfectly, I felt like a complete failure.

- **Overgeneralization:** Making broad interpretations from a single or few events. After one bad day, I'd think, "I'll never have a good day again."

- **Catastrophizing:** Expecting the worst-case scenario. If something minor went wrong, I'd immediately think it was the end of the world.

Understanding these distortions helped me realize that my thinking was skewed and that these thoughts were not reflective of reality. Cognitive-behavioral therapy (CBT) provided tools to challenge and reframe these negative thoughts, leading to a significant improvement in my mood and outlook.

Learned Helplessness

The concept of learned helplessness, introduced by psychologist Martin Seligman in the 1970s, provides another lens through which to understand depression. Learned helplessness occurs when individuals believe they have no control over their circumstances and thus stop trying to change their situation, even when opportunities for change exist.

Seligman's initial experiments involved dogs that were subjected to unavoidable shocks. Eventually, the dogs stopped trying to escape the shocks, even when they were later placed in a situation where escape was possible. This behavior was termed "learned helplessness."

In humans, learned helplessness can develop after repeated exposure to stressful or uncontrollable situations. For me, this manifested in an inescapable sense of defeat and resignation. After numerous setbacks and failures, I began to feel that no matter what I did, nothing would change for the better. This led to a lack of motivation and an acceptance of my depressive state as unchangeable.

Learning about learned helplessness was both eye-opening and empowering. It made me realize that my feelings of helplessness were learned responses and that, with effort and support, I could unlearn them. Therapy and gradual exposure to new, controllable experiences helped me regain a sense of agency and hope.

Psychoanalytic Perspectives

While cognitive-behavioral and learned helplessness theories focus on present thought patterns and behaviors, psychoanalytic perspectives venture into the unconscious mind and past experiences to explain depression. Developed by Sigmund Freud and later expanded by others, psychoanalytic theory suggests that unresolved conflicts and repressed emotions from childhood can contribute to depression.

According to Freud, depression can result from unresolved grief or loss. He believed that individuals with depression often direct feelings of anger and guilt towards themselves, leading to self-punishment and low self-esteem. For example, a person who experienced significant loss or neglect in childhood might internalize these feelings, leading to crippling sadness and self-criticism in adulthood.

Object Relations Theory: Later psychoanalytic theorists, such as Melanie Klein and Donald Winnicott, emphasized the importance of early relationships in shaping one's self-concept and emotional health. They suggested that dysfunctional early relationships could lead to difficulties in forming secure attachments, contributing to depression. In my case, reflecting on past relationships and understanding their impact on my self-worth and emotional patterns provided valuable insights into my depressive tendencies.

Psychoanalytic therapy, often involving long-term exploration of one's past and unconscious mind, aims to bring these hidden conflicts to light. Through this process, individuals can work through unresolved issues and develop healthier ways of relating to themselves and others. For me, this deep introspection was challenging but ultimately liberating, helping me to understand the roots of my depression and find ways to heal.

While each of these theories offers valuable insights, it's important to recognize that depression is multifaceted, and no single theory can fully explain it. An integrative approach, combining elements from various theories, often provides the most comprehensive understanding and effective treatment. Cognitive-behavioral techniques can help reframe negative thinking patterns, while insights from psychoanalytic therapy can address deeper, underlying issues. Recognizing and addressing learned helplessness can empower individuals to take control of their lives and make positive changes.

Embracing this integrative approach has been awe-inspiring for my own recovery. It has allowed me to tackle depression from multiple angles, addressing both immediate symptoms and deeper-rooted issues. This holistic understanding has informed my treatment choices and built a sense of empathy and self-compassion. As we continue exploring the biology and psychology of depression, it becomes evident that a comprehensive approach is essential for effective treatment and lasting recovery.

Past traumas often comprise a significant part in shaping our experiences of depression. Trauma and depression are often threaded together, with the former acting as a catalyst for the latter. In his groundbreaking book, **"The Body Keeps the Score**," Dr. Bessel van der Kolk explains how traumatic experiences can leave lasting imprints on our bodies and minds, influencing our emotional well-being long after the events have passed.

Trauma, whether it stems from childhood abuse, neglect, or significant life events such as accidents or loss, disrupts the body's natural ability to process and integrate experiences. Van der Kolk explains that trauma can alter brain function, particularly in areas responsible for fear, stress regulation, and emotional control. These changes can make individuals more susceptible to depression, as their brains become wired to expect danger and distress even in safe environments.

When we experience trauma, our bodies go into a heightened state of arousal, preparing to fight, flee, or freeze. This response is driven by the release of stress hormones like cortisol and adrenaline. In normal circumstances, once the threat passes, our bodies return to a state of equilibrium. However, trauma can disrupt this process, causing a constant state of hyperarousal or numbness. This persistent stress response can lead to chronic anxiety, insomnia, and ultimately, depression. I remember feeling constantly on edge, my body never truly relaxing, even in moments of supposed calm.

Trauma often leads to fragmented and disorganized memories. Instead of being stored as coherent narratives, traumatic experiences can be split into isolated sensory fragments. This disorganization can make it difficult to process and integrate the trauma, leading to intrusive memories and flashbacks. Van der Kolk describes how these fragmented memories can resurface unexpectedly, triggering intense emotional reactions and reinforcing feelings of helplessness and despair. For years, certain sounds or smells would transport me back to traumatic moments, causing a flood of emotions that felt uncontrollable.

The title of van der Kolk's book, "The Body Keeps the Score," encapsulates the idea that our bodies remember trauma even when our conscious minds do not. Trauma can manifest in physical symptoms such as chronic pain, gastrointestinal issues, and fatigue, all of which can contribute to or exacerbate depression. Understanding this connection was transformational for me. Realizing that my physical symptoms were linked to past traumas helped me approach my depression more holistically, addressing both my mind and body in the healing process.

Childhood Trauma and Its Legacy

Childhood trauma, in particular, has a major impact on the development of depression. Adverse childhood experiences (ACEs) such as abuse, neglect, and household dysfunction are strongly correlated with mental health issues in adulthood. The ACE study, conducted by the Centers for Disease Control and Prevention (CDC) and Kaiser Permanente, found that individuals with higher ACE scores were more likely to suffer from depression, anxiety, and other mental health disorders.

Early attachment relationships heavily contribute to shaping our ability to regulate emotions. Secure attachments with caregivers provide a foundation of safety and trust, enabling children to develop healthy coping mechanisms. Conversely, inconsistent or harmful caregiving can disrupt this process, leading to difficulties in emotional regulation and increased vulnerability to depression. Van der Kolk highlights how children who grow up in chaotic or abusive environments often struggle with self-soothing and are more likely to experience chronic stress and depression later in life. Personally, I had responsive and caring parents that ensured that I wasn't neglected. However, my experiences of inconsistency and neglect in childhood stemmed from the fact that they did not understand what I was going through and how I was gradually developing a crippling depression which threw me into a cave of isolation and loneliness. This caused a lingering sense of insecurity and emotional instability, disconnecting me from my caregivers despite not being conventionally traumatized.

In addition, childhood trauma can also distort an individual's sense of self. Negative messages from caregivers or peers, coupled with traumatic experiences, can lead to internalized beliefs of worthlessness and inadequacy. These beliefs can persist into adulthood, forming a core component of depressive thinking. For years, I carried the weight of these internalized messages, feeling inherently flawed and undeserving of happiness.

Trauma Reenactment and Relational Patterns

Subsequently, trauma doesn't just stay in the past; it often gets reenacted in present relationships and behaviors. This phenomenon, known as "trauma reenactment," can perpetuate cycles of depression and dysfunction. Individuals may unconsciously recreate aspects of their trauma, seeking out relationships or situations that mirror their past experiences.

Van der Kolk explains that trauma survivors often find themselves in situations that replicate their original trauma. This can be a way of attempting to gain mastery over the trauma or because the familiar, even if painful, feels safer than the unknown. For example, someone who experienced abuse might find themselves in abusive relationships as an adult, reinforcing their feelings of helplessness and despair. Recognizing these patterns in your life can be a turning point. It allows you to break free from cycles of reenactment and seek healthier, more supportive relationships.

Another common response to trauma is 'Dissociation', where individuals disconnect from their thoughts, feelings, or sense of identity to cope with overwhelming stress. While dissociation can provide temporary relief, it can also contribute to depression by preventing the processing and integration of traumatic memories. Van der Kolk describes how dissociation can lead to a fragmented sense of self, making it difficult to experience a cohesive and fulfilling life. During my depressive episodes, I often felt disconnected from myself and my surroundings, as if I were living in a fog. This went forth for a considerable period of time and remained a material issue that I struggled with throughout my struggle with mental health.

Healing from Trauma

For effective healing, it is essential to embody an approach that addresses both the psychological and physiological impacts of trauma. Van der Kolk advocates for therapies that integrate body and mind, such as:

Trauma-Focused Therapy: Trauma-focused cognitive-behavioral therapy (TF-CBT) and Eye Movement Desensitization and Reprocessing (EMDR) are designed to help individuals process and integrate traumatic memories. These therapies work by gradually exposing individuals to traumatic memories in a safe and controlled environment, allowing them to reprocess these memories and reduce their emotional impact.

Somatic Experiencing: Somatic experiencing focuses on the body's physiological responses to trauma. By working with the body, this approach helps individuals release stored tension and complete the stress response cycle. Techniques such as grounding exercises, mindfulness, and body awareness are used to reconnect individuals with their physical sensations and promote healing. Incorporating body-focused therapies into your treatment plan can be a transformative experience.

It helps you to reconnect with your body and release the tension that has been stored for years.

Mindfulness and Yoga: Mindfulness practices and yoga can also be effective in treating trauma-related depression. These practices promote body awareness, relaxation, and a sense of control over one's body and mind. Van der Kolk emphasizes the importance of creating a sense of safety and agency, which can be fostered through regular mindfulness and yoga practices. Engaging in these practices provided me with a sense of grounding and stability, helping me manage my depressive symptoms more effectively. In fact, to this day, I have continued with these practices to not only fight with mental illnesses but to turn my mental health into a beacon of light and hope.

Understanding your trauma and its impact on depression can be a groundbreaking part of your healing journey. It will allow you to approach depression with greater compassion and a more comprehensive strategy. I've been able to make significant strides towards recovery by addressing the psychological, physiological, and relational aspects of trauma. So can you. So can they. So can anyone.

Marching on with our journey to understand biology and psychology of depression, it becomes clear that a holistic approach is essential. Trauma and depression are deeply needled, and healing requires addressing both the mind and body. In the next section, we will look into the latest research and insights into depression, exploring how genetic studies and innovative therapies are shedding new light on this deplorable condition.

NEW RESEARCH AND INSIGHTS

The field of depression research is continually evolving, generating new insights and innovative therapies that hold promise for better understanding and treating this horrendous condition. Advances in genetic studies, neuroimaging, and novel therapeutic approaches are shedding light on the intricate mechanisms of depression and opening new pathways for treatment.

Genetic Studies and Depression

As understood earlier, genetics encumber a central role in depression, influencing susceptibility and individual responses to treatment. Recent genetic studies have identified numerous genetic variants associated with depression, providing a deeper understanding of its biological underpinnings.

Genetic Risk Factors: Genome-wide association studies (GWAS) have identified several genetic loci linked to depression. These studies examine the entire genome to identify genetic variations that occur more frequently in individuals with depression compared to those without. For example, research has highlighted the involvement of the gene SLC6A4, which codes for the serotonin transporter. Variations in this gene can affect serotonin levels in the brain, influencing mood regulation and susceptibility to depression.

Another significant finding is the identification of the gene CACNA1C, which is involved in calcium signaling in neurons. Variations in this gene have been associated with both depression and bipolar disorder, suggesting a shared genetic risk factor for mood disorders. These discoveries highlight the complexity of depression, involving multiple genes and biological pathways.

Epigenetics: Epigenetics, the study of changes in gene expression without altering the underlying DNA sequence, is another exciting area of research. Environmental factors, such as stress and trauma, can modify gene expression through epigenetic mechanisms, potentially contributing to the development of depression. For instance, studies have shown that early-life stress can lead to epigenetic changes in the glucocorticoid receptor gene, affecting the body's stress response and increasing the risk of depression later in life.

Understanding these epigenetic changes opens up possibilities for targeted interventions that could reverse or mitigate the impact of adverse environmental influences. This area of research highlights the dynamic interplay between genes and the environment in shaping mental health.

Neuroimaging and Brain Structure Changes

Neuroimaging technologies, such as functional magnetic resonance imaging (fMRI) and positron emission tomography (PET), have transformed our understanding of the brain's role in depression. These tools allow researchers to observe brain activity and structural changes in real-time, providing valuable insights into the neural mechanisms underlying depression.

Brain Regions Involved: Neuroimaging studies have consistently identified abnormalities in specific brain regions associated with depression. The prefrontal cortex, responsible for executive functions and decision-making, often shows reduced activity in individuals with depression. This reduced activity can impair cognitive functions such as concentration and decision-making, contributing to the cognitive symptoms of depression.

The amygdala, a key region involved in emotion processing, often exhibits heightened activity in response to negative stimuli in depressed individuals. This heightened reactivity can lead to an increased focus on negative emotions and experiences, reinforcing depressive thoughts and feelings. Additionally, the hippocampus, involved in memory formation, often shows reduced volume in individuals with chronic depression. This reduction in volume is thought to result from the prolonged exposure to stress hormones, which can damage hippocampal neurons.

Neuroplasticity: Recent research has demonstrated the role of neuroplasticity, the brain's ability to adapt and reorganize itself, in depression. Depression is associated with reduced neuroplasticity, particularly in the hippocampus and prefrontal cortex. Treatments that enhance neuroplasticity, such as antidepressants and certain forms of psychotherapy, can help restore normal brain function and alleviate depressive symptoms.

For instance, studies have shown that selective serotonin reuptake inhibitors (SSRIs) can promote neurogenesis, the formation of new neurons, in the hippocampus. This process is thought to contribute to the therapeutic effects of antidepressants, supporting the idea that enhancing neuroplasticity can be a key strategy in treating depression.

Innovative Therapies

As our understanding of depression deepens, new and innovative therapies are emerging that offer hope for more effective and personalized treatments.

Ketamine and Esketamine: Ketamine, a medication traditionally used as an anesthetic, has gained attention for its rapid antidepressant effects. Unlike traditional antidepressants, which can take weeks to become effective, ketamine can alleviate depressive symptoms within hours. Ketamine works by blocking NMDA receptors in the brain, leading to increased levels of the neurotransmitter glutamate and promoting synaptic growth and connectivity.

Esketamine, a derivative of ketamine, has been approved by the FDA for treatment-resistant depression. Administered as a nasal spray, esketamine provides a new option for individuals who have not responded to conventional treatments. The rapid action of ketamine and esketamine represents a significant breakthrough, offering relief for those experiencing severe and acute depressive episodes.

Transcranial Magnetic Stimulation (TMS): TMS is a non-invasive procedure that uses magnetic fields to stimulate nerve cells in the brain. TMS targets specific brain regions, such as the prefrontal cortex, to modulate neural activity and improve depressive symptoms. This treatment has shown promise for individuals with treatment-resistant depression, providing an alternative to medication and traditional therapy. TMS is typically administered over several weeks, with sessions lasting about 30 minutes. The targeted nature of TMS allows for precise modulation of brain activity, minimizing side effects and offering a promising option for those who have not found relief with other treatments.

Psilocybin Therapy: Psilocybin, the active compound in psychedelic mushrooms, is being studied for its potential therapeutic effects in depression. Preliminary research suggests that psilocybin can produce profound and lasting improvements in mood and well-being, particularly in individuals with treatment-resistant depression. Psilocybin therapy involves guided sessions with trained therapists, where individuals consume the compound in a controlled setting. The psychedelic experience induced by psilocybin is thought to facilitate emotional processing and cognitive flexibility, helping individuals gain new perspectives on their thoughts and feelings. While more research is needed, early results are promising, indicating that psilocybin could be a valuable addition to the therapeutic arsenal for depression.

Personalized Medicine: Advances in genetics and neuroimaging are paving the way for personalized medicine in depression treatment. By understanding an individual's unique genetic makeup and brain function, clinicians can tailor treatments to maximize effectiveness and minimize side effects. For example, pharmacogenetic testing can identify how a person metabolizes certain medications, allowing for more precise prescribing practices. Personalized approaches also extend to psychotherapy, where treatments can be customized based on an individual's specific psychological profile and history. This approach ensures that interventions are targeted and relevant, enhancing the likelihood of successful outcomes.

The rapid advancements in depression research are transforming our understanding of this condition and offering new hope for effective treatments. Genetic studies, neuroimaging, and innovative therapies are shedding light on the nuanced mechanisms underlying depression, paving the path for more personalized and effective interventions.

In the pursuit of any treatment and cure, it is always imperative to remain open to new findings and approaches. The cross between genetic, neurological, and psychological factors calls the need for a comprehensive and integrative approach to treatment. We can develop more effective strategies to alleviate the burden of depression and improve the lives of those affected by keeping up with the latest research and insights.

Depression is a shadow that can darken every corner of one's life, often making the idea of living unbearable. For many, the crushing weight of depression can lead to thoughts of suicide. The link between depression and suicide is deep and alarming. When the hopelessness and despair of depression become overwhelming, suicide can seem like the only way to escape the pain. Learning about this critical link is not just about identifying risk factors and warning signs; it's about recognizing the depth of suffering that can lead someone to consider ending their own life.

Suicide is a complicated issue with many faces, but one of the most significant risk factors is severe depression. The emotional and psychological pain experienced during a major depressive episode can be so intense that it eclipses all other thoughts and feelings. It's not simply a desire to die, but rather an overwhelming urge to end the pain. This distinction is the bedrock of understanding why someone might consider suicide as an option. For those who have never experienced depression, it's difficult to comprehend how all-encompassing the despair can be. It's as if the mind is trapped in a dark tunnel with no light at the end.

The link between depression and suicide becomes truly illuminated when we consider its prevalence. According to the World Health Organization, more than 264 million people worldwide suffer from depression, and close to 800,000 people die by suicide each year. This statistic shows the urgent need to address depression as a major public health issue. While not everyone who experiences depression will contemplate suicide, those with severe depression are at a significantly higher risk.

The journey from depression to suicidal thoughts is often a gradual one. It begins with feelings of worthlessness and hopelessness, which can escalate to a belief that life is not worth living. As these thoughts intensify, they can become more specific and urgent, leading to suicidal ideation. It's essential to understand that suicidal thoughts are not a sign of weakness or a character flaw; they are a symptom of a serious mental health condition that requires attention and treatment.

One of the most heartbreaking aspects of this connection is that many who die by suicide do so in a state of deep isolation and despair. They feel misunderstood, unsupported, or a burden to their loved ones. The stigma surrounding mental health exacerbates these feelings, making it difficult for individuals to reach out and seek help. This isolation only deepens their sense of hopelessness, creating a vicious cycle that can be hard to break.

Personal stories of those who have struggled with depression and suicidal thoughts are particularly illuminating, casting light on a dark subject. My own struggles with depression have brought me to the brink multiple times. Each attempt was not about wanting to die but about wanting the pain to stop. It's an excruciating place to be, where every breath feels heavy and every moment is filled with dread. Surviving those moments requires immense strength and support, which not everyone has access to. I was lucky. I am lucky.

This chapter talks about the delicate and often devastating relationship between depression and suicide. It will explore the risk factors that increase the likelihood of suicidal thoughts and behaviors, identify the warning signs that may indicate someone is in crisis, and discuss intervention strategies to provide support and prevent suicide. Finally, we will address the aftermath of suicide attempts, focusing on coping mechanisms for survivors and their families. Understanding this link is not just a matter of academic interest; it's a matter of saving lives. By shedding light on these dark corners, we can offer hope and support to those who are struggling, showing them that they are not alone and that there is a way out of the tunnel. I have been through one end and out the other. There is, undoubtedly, light at the end of the tunnel.

SUICIDE RISK FACTORS

Suicide is a chilling word, one that carries the weight of ultimate despair. The risk factors for suicide are entangled, intertwining biological, psychological, and social elements. In understanding these factors, we can better identify those at risk and intervene effectively. While it's practically impossible to predict with certainty who will attempt suicide, recognizing the signs and underlying issues can save lives.

As you may have guessed, one significant risk factor is severe depression. Major depressive disorder can cloud the mind, leading to a sense of hopelessness and despair that feels inescapable. During the darkest periods of my own depression, the thought of ending the pain permanently was a constant, haunting presence. Severe depression can render a person almost catatonic, where even the simplest tasks, like getting out of bed or brushing teeth, seem insurmountable. During these times, the risk of suicide is paradoxically lower because the individual lacks the energy to act on suicidal thoughts.

However, the danger intensifies as the person begins to recover. This might sound counterintuitive, but as someone who has been there, I can attest to its truth. When depression starts to lift, the individual regains enough energy and cognitive function to follow through on suicidal impulses that may have been festering. This period of recovery, where "psychomotor retardation" begins to ease, is when vigilance is most necessary.

I remember a time when I was hospitalized for severe depression. Lying in that hospital bed, every movement felt like dragging a weight behind me. Even lifting my head was an effort. The hospital staff were less concerned about me doing something drastic then because they knew I physically couldn't. It was when I started to feel a little better, when I could muster enough strength to move around, that they watched me more closely. I had the energy but still carried the darkness within me. This is a critical window where intervention can be lifesaving.

Previous suicide attempts are another powerful risk factor. A past attempt significantly increases the likelihood of future attempts. Each attempt indicates a depth of despair that requires serious and sustained intervention. When I survived my own attempts, it wasn't just a matter of getting through that moment. It was about acknowledging the persistent risk and finding long-term strategies to manage it. Every subsequent day felt like walking on a tightrope, balancing between hope and despair. The scars from those attempts were not just physical; they were etched into my very being, a constant reminder of how close I had come.

Family history is also work here. Genetic predispositions to mood disorders and suicidal behavior can create a heightened risk environment. Growing up in a family where depression and suicide attempts were present, I saw firsthand how these issues could pervade generations. I **was** that generation. It felt like an unspoken curse, a shadow that loomed over every family gathering. Understanding this genetic link helped me realize that my struggles were not just my own; they were part of a larger, more complex family narrative. Recognizing this can be a double-edged sword. On one hand, it brings a sense of shared experience, but on the other, it can feel like an inescapable destiny. However, I must say, it is imperative to remember, genetics are an influence, not destiny.

Co-occurring mental health conditions, such as anxiety disorders, bipolar disorder, and substance abuse, further complicate the risk profile. The interaction between these conditions can intensify feelings of hopelessness and impulsivity. During my darkest periods, anxiety constantly fed into my depression, creating a vicious cycle. The panic attacks, the constant sense of impending doom, layered over the deep sadness, made every day a struggle. Substance abuse, often used as a coping mechanism, can lower inhibitions and increase the likelihood of acting on suicidal thoughts. The numbing effects of alcohol or drugs might offer temporary relief, but they ultimately deepen the sense of despair and isolation.

Apart from being symptoms, chronic pain and serious medical conditions are also risk factors. The relentless nature of chronic pain can erode one's will to live, making the idea of ending the suffering seem appealing. I've known people who faced this dual battle, dealing with both physical and emotional pain. Their stories echoed a common theme: the relentless search for relief. Serious medical conditions, particularly those that limit one's independence or quality of life, can lead to a deep sense of loss and hopelessness. It's not just the physical ailment but the perceived loss of identity and future that can drive someone to consider suicide.

Social isolation and lack of support are critical elements that can push someone towards the brink. We humans are inherently social beings, and the absence of meaningful connections can exacerbate feelings of worthlessness and despair. During my depressive episodes, the isolation was palpable. Friends drifted away, unable to understand or cope with my darkness. Family members, despite their love, mostly felt helpless. This isolation creates a feedback loop where the lack of support deepens the depression, which in turn drives further isolation. It's a silent killer, one that thrives in the shadows of loneliness.

Economic hardship and financial stress are also significant triggers. The constant worry about bills, job security, and future prospects can weigh heavily on someone already battling depression. Financial instability can erode self-esteem and create a sense of helplessness. Whom of us haven't been there? Staring at a stack (or a pdf) of unpaid bills, feeling burdened with responsibility. The pressure of providing for oneself or one's family, combined with the fear of losing everything, can be overwhelming, especially for the providers of a household. It's a relentless burden that can make the idea of escape through suicide seem like the only viable option.

The cultural and societal factors must also not be ignored. In some cultures, the stigma surrounding mental health issues and suicide can prevent individuals from seeking help. The pressure to conform to societal norms and the fear of being judged can lead to secrecy and isolation. I've encountered people from various backgrounds who struggled in silence because their culture, including mine, viewed mental illness as a weakness, if even viewed it at all. This cultural barrier can be a formidable obstacle to getting the necessary help and support. This plays directly into the hands of social isolation and exclusion.

Recognizing and understanding these risk factors is about seeing the whole person, acknowledging their pain, and providing the support they need. Even if that person is you, yourself. As we move forward, we'll explore the warning signs of suicidal behavior and the strategies for intervening and offering help. This journey through understanding suicide risk is not just about identifying those at risk but about creating a compassionate and supportive environment where they feel seen, heard, and valued. We can offer a lifeline in their darkest moments by acknowledging the depth of their struggle, showing them that they are not alone and that there is hope beyond the pain.

WARNING SIGNS

Warning signs of suicidal intent are hard to recognize. They are like being able to read the subtle shifts in weather before a storm. The signs are usually faint and easily dismissed, but their presence can signify an approaching crisis. Being attuned to these cues makes the difference between life and death.

Behavioral Cues

Behavioral changes are often the first and most visible indicators that something is wrong. When I was at my lowest, my actions spoke louder than my words. I remember canceling plans with friends and skipping family gatherings. Isolation is a significant red flag. A person who suddenly withdraws from social activities they once enjoyed might be signaling that they feel overwhelmed or disconnected. It's not just about being alone but about avoiding the very connections that might offer support. I understand that a person may choose to do so without being suicidal, but isn't it always better to be vigilant and compassionate than lose yourself in the aftermath of "What Ifs"?

Another behavioral sign is a sudden, inexplicable calm after a period of intense depression. This can be a chilling indicator that the person has made a decision to end their life, providing a temporary sense of relief. This calmness is not to be mistaken for recovery. I've been there, on the precipice, feeling an eerie peace after deciding to act on my suicidal thoughts. It felt like the weight of decision-making had lifted, and all that was left was to follow through.

When looking for these signs, look for changes in routine and personal care. Neglecting personal hygiene, failing to keep up with work or school responsibilities, and a general decline in daily functioning are all signs that the person is struggling. I went from meticulously planning my schoolwork to barely being able to get dressed. This deterioration is not just about losing interest; it's about losing the capacity to care.

Similarly. giving away prized possessions is another significant behavioral cue. It might seem like a generous act, but it often indicates that the person is preparing for their absence. Personally, I didn't have any prized possessions, I think. But if I had, I think I would have handed over my favorite books to someone. It isn't a random act of kindness; it is often a goodbye.

Risky behaviors can also be a cry for help. Increased use of alcohol or drugs, reckless driving, or other dangerous activities may signal that the person is in turmoil. These actions often reflect a disregard for personal safety and a subconscious desire to escape pain, even if it's through dangerous means. During my darkest times, I found myself taking risks I never would have considered before. It was a way of tempting fate, of testing the boundaries of my existence. I used to test my boundaries further and further every time, hoping that fate would make a decision for me. It's almost like giving up control.

Verbal Cues

Verbal cues can be more challenging to detect because they often hide in plain sight. They can range from direct statements of intent to subtle hints cloaked in everyday conversation. Recognizing these cues requires a keen ear and a willingness to delve deeper into what's being said.

Direct statements like, "I wish I were dead," or "I can't take this anymore," are clear indicators of suicidal intent. These declarations should never be taken lightly, no matter how casual they may sound. I've uttered these words myself, hoping someone would notice and intervene. When someone expresses these thoughts, it's a plea for help, a final attempt to reach out before slipping into the abyss. Do not let them slide over without compassionate attention.

More subtle hints can be just as telling. Phrases like, "You'd be better off without me," or "What's the point of anything?" indicate a deep sense of hopelessness and worthlessness.

These statements reflect an internal struggle, a belief that their existence is a burden to others. Telling a friend, "You deserve better friends than me" may not just be a casual sentence but rather a reflection of what's going inside someone's mind. It is often a way of expressing that I feel like a burden, that my presence is more of a curse than a blessing.

Conversations about death and dying, even in a seemingly abstract or philosophical context, can be a sign of suicidal ideation. If someone frequently talks about the afterlife, funerals, or ways people die, it might indicate that they are contemplating these ideas more seriously than they let on. During some of my conversations, I would steer the topic towards death, masked as philosophical musings, when in reality, I was seeking validation for my thoughts.

Expressions of hopelessness are another verbal cue. When someone says, "There's no way out," or "Things will never get better," it reveals a belief that their situation is unchangeable. This sense of hopelessness is a hallmark of suicidal ideation. It's not just about feeling sad; it's about believing that there is no possibility of a future worth living. I've felt this crushing hopelessness, convinced that my pain was eternal and escape was the only option. I never thought I would live past a certain age, just like so many others like me.

Talking about feeling trapped or being in unbearable pain is a cry for help. These expressions are about more than just physical pain; they encompass emotional and psychological suffering. Statements like, "I can't escape this," or "The pain is too much," are indicators that the person feels overwhelmed and sees no other way out. Saying, "I feel trapped in my own mind," may not be the casual remark we often contemplate it to be. It might be someone hoping to be understood through severe anguish.

Interpreting the Signs

Understanding these cues demands empathy, attentiveness, and a willingness to act. It's about seeing beyond the surface and recognizing the deeper struggle. When someone shows these signs, it's not an overreaction to intervene; it's a necessary step to potentially save a life.

The most compassionate thing someone has ever done for me was when my friend noticed my behavioral changes and persistent verbal hints. Instead of brushing them off, she addressed them and asked me directly about my thoughts. It was uncomfortable and raw, but it was also life-saving. Her willingness to see the signs and address them directly gave me the space to express my pain and seek help. Now that I think of it, it might have been the initiation of my journey toward healing.

Recognizing these warning signs is not just the responsibility of mental health professionals but of everyone in the community. Friends, family members, colleagues, and even casual acquaintances can exhibit an integral role in identifying and addressing these cues. It's about creating a culture where mental health is openly discussed, and support is readily available.

Intervening when someone shows signs of suicidal intent is an act of profound compassion. It requires courage to ask the difficult questions and offer unwavering support. It's about being present, listening without judgment, and providing a safe space for the person to express their pain.

Learning about these warning signs can pave the way for timely intervention. It's about being vigilant, compassionate, and proactive in offering help. Every sign is a chance to make a difference, to offer hope, and to show that no one has to face their darkest moments alone. Through awareness and action, we can create a lifeline for those on the brink, guiding them back towards the light and a future filled with possibilities. However, I must emphasize, you can always be your own light as well.

SELF-HARM

Now before we move on any further, I want to talk about a rarely talked topic, Self-harm. Self-harm, also known as self-injury or self-mutilation, is a deeply distressing behavior that often accompanies severe depression and other mental health issues. It involves deliberately inflicting pain or injury on oneself, typically as a way to cope with intense emotional distress. Even though this behavior is not a suicide attempt but rather a maladaptive strategy to manage overwhelming feelings, I felt compelled to talk about it here. This is because understanding self-harm can give us an idea of recognizing the depths of someone's emotional pain and providing appropriate support.

Self-harm can take many forms, including cutting, burning, scratching, or hitting oneself. For some, it might involve more subtle methods like pulling out hair or picking at wounds to prevent healing. Each act of self-injury serves as a physical manifestation of emotional pain, a desperate attempt to exert control over one's suffering. When I was in the throes of my deepest depression, self-harm became a secret ritual, a way to externalize the unbearable internal turmoil. The physical pain, in a twisted way, was a relief; it was tangible, something I could manage in a world that felt utterly uncontrollable. It wasn't about wanting to die; it was about wanting to feel something other than the crushing emotional numbness. I can still touch my scars, and feel shivers down my spine. They're a dark reminder of a dark past.

The impulse to self-harm is complex and does not arise from a single factor but many. For most, it's about release; an immediate way to alleviate intense emotions. The physical pain can momentarily distract from the emotional anguish, creating a temporary sense of relief. This relief is often short-lived, leading to an unfortunate cycle of shame and further self-injury.

One common trigger for self-harm is feeling overwhelmed by emotions. When sadness, anger, or anxiety becomes too much to bear, causing physical pain can serve as a release valve. It's a way to express feelings that seem inexpressible through words alone. For instance, I often found myself drawn to cutting as a way to channel my helplessness and despair. Each cut was a mark to my internal struggle, a way to make the invisible visible.

Another driving force behind self-harm is a sense of self-punishment. Feelings of worthlessness and guilt can lead individuals to believe they deserve pain. This is often compounded by negative self-talk and cognitive distortions that convince them they are a burden to others. The urge to self-harm often comes when you feel that you have failed in some way; failed yourself, failed others. The physical pain feels like atonement, a way to pay for perceived shortcomings.

This act of self-harm triggers the release of endorphins, the body's natural painkillers. These chemicals can create a feeling of euphoria or calm, reinforcing the behavior. This biological response can make self-harm addictive, as individuals seek out the endorphin rush to cope with their emotional pain. The science behind this is both fascinating and frightening. When you injure yourself, your body responds by flooding your system with endorphins to numb the pain. This rush can provide a momentary high, a break from the relentless emotional suffering. However, it's a dangerous cycle because the relief is fleeting, and the need for a more intense release can grow, leading to increasingly severe self-harm behaviors.

Watching my own cuts form felt as it may feel to many; cathartic, but all I can think of now, is how painful it must have been for me, as it is for many, and how much better it should have been handled by me and everyone around me; as it should be by you and everyone else around you. It should never have come down to it. But Alas! I know better now, and hope that by the end of this book, so will you.

Recognizing the Signs

Recognizing the signs of self-harm can be challenging because individuals often go to great lengths to hide their injuries. However, there are subtle clues that can indicate someone is engaging in self-injury.

One of the most telling signs is wearing long sleeves or pants, even in warm weather, to cover up cuts or bruises. This was my go-to strategy; I'd layer up, even on sweltering days, to keep my secret hidden. Additionally, individuals might avoid activities that require revealing clothing, such as swimming or changing in front of others. It wasn't until I faced my demons that I started comfortable enough to start rolling up my sleeves.

Frequent, unexplained injuries are another red flag. If someone has a pattern of injuries they can't convincingly explain; like frequent cuts or burns, it's worth paying attention. These injuries might be passed off as accidents, but their repetitive nature often hints at something more deliberate.

Changes in behavior like increased irritability, withdrawal from social interactions, and declining academic or work performance can all be indicators. In my case, my behavior became erratic and unpredictable. I'd isolate myself for days, avoiding friends and family to keep my injuries hidden and to indulge in destructive behavior without interference.

Coming across tools or objects associated with self-harm can be an alarming indicator. Discovering razors, lighters, or sharp objects in unusual places might suggest that someone is using them to self-injure. I had a stash of tools hidden away, always ready for when the urge struck. It became a ritualistic part of my coping mechanism.

The Psychological Impact

The psychological impact of self-harm is deep and piercing. While it might provide temporary relief, it often leads to feelings of shame, guilt, and isolation. The physical scars are a constant reminder of emotional pain, reinforcing a negative self-image and perpetuating the cycle of self-injury.

Self-harm also complicates relationships. Loved ones might struggle to understand the behavior, feeling helpless and frustrated. This can lead to strained relationships and further isolation for the individual. In my experience, those closest to me didn't understand why I was hurting myself. Their confusion and worry often turned into frustration, which only deepened my sense of isolation.

Moreover, the secrecy surrounding self-harm can prevent individuals from seeking help. The fear of judgment and stigma keeps many from reaching out, allowing the behavior to continue unchecked. It is a terrifying thought among the afflicted to be labeled as "crazy" or "attention-seeking," and so just like many, I kept my pain to myself, sinking deeper into my dark abyss.

Self-harm is a destructive behavior rooted in deep emotional pain, serving as a maladaptive coping mechanism for many. We can support those in pain with their journey toward healing by recognizing the signs, offering empathy, and encouraging professional help. It doesn't take much on our part, but will change their lives, and our world.

I now realize the importance of breaking the silence surrounding self-harm. Sharing our stories can reduce stigma, nurture understanding, and offer hope to those still battling their inner demons. Through awareness and compassionate intervention, we can help those struggling with self-harm find healthier ways to cope and begin their journey toward recovery. I keep reiterating my personal experiences because I realize that understanding depression is not an easy task, especially for those who haven't struggled with mental illnesses themselves, and maybe hearing these memoirs will invoke a sense of empathy in a single person that leads to a single person being eased off of their pain.

INTERVENTION STRATEGIES

When someone you care about might be contemplating suicide, it can be an incredibly daunting and emotional situation. Knowing how to approach and support them effectively is essential. Your actions can make the difference between life and death, offering hope and help when it is most needed.

Starting the conversation about suicide requires a delicate balance of empathy, directness, and sensitivity. It's important to approach the person in a private, comfortable setting where they feel safe and free from interruptions.

1. **Be Direct but Compassionate**: It's a common misconception that asking someone about suicidal thoughts will put the idea in their head. In reality, asking directly about their feelings can provide relief and show them that you are genuinely concerned. You might say, "I've noticed you seem really down lately, and I'm worried about you. Are you thinking about hurting yourself?" This direct approach signals that you are taking their pain seriously.

2. **Express Your Concerns**: Use "I" statements to convey your feelings without sounding accusatory. For example, "I've been feeling concerned about you lately. You don't seem like yourself, and I want to help." This

method helps to avoid putting them on the defensive and keeps the focus on your care and concern.

3. **Listen Actively**: This is perhaps the most vital aspect. Listen without judgment, interruptions, or immediate solutions. Sometimes, the person just needs to feel heard and understood. Nodding, maintaining eye contact, and providing verbal affirmations like "I'm here for you" or "I understand this is hard" can make a significant impact.

4. **Validate Their Feelings**: Avoid dismissing their emotions or offering platitudes. Instead of saying, "Things aren't that bad," acknowledge their feelings with, "I can see how much pain you're in right now." This validation can help them feel understood and less isolated in their suffering.

Once the conversation is underway, offering tangible support can help the individual feel less overwhelmed and more hopeful.

1. **Ask How You Can Help**: Everyone's needs are different, so it's essential to ask what kind of support they need. They might want someone to talk to, help with daily tasks, or assistance in finding professional help.

2. **Encourage Professional Help**: Gently suggest seeking professional support, such as a therapist or counselor. You could say, "Talking to a therapist has helped me when I've felt overwhelmed. Would you be open to seeing someone?" Offer to help them find a therapist or go with them to their first appointment if they're anxious about it.

3. **Create a Safety Plan**: Work together to develop a safety plan. This can include removing access to means of self-harm, such as medications, sharp objects, or

firearms. Additionally, identify emergency contacts and local crisis resources. Discuss what they can do when they feel overwhelmed, like calling a friend or crisis hotline.

4. **Check In Regularly**: Continue to check in on them frequently. Regular contact shows that you care and are there for them, helping to reduce their feelings of isolation. Even a quick text or phone call can make a big difference.

Always remember that supporting someone who is suicidal is very challenging, and recognizing your own limits is essential. You can offer support and encouragement, but you cannot single-handedly resolve their issues.

1. **Set Boundaries**: It's important to set boundaries to protect your own mental health. Supporting someone in crisis can be emotionally draining, and you need to ensure you're also taking care of yourself. Explain that while you're there for them, they might also need additional support from professionals.

2. **Seek Support for Yourself**: Don't hesitate to seek guidance for yourself. Talking to a counselor or joining a support group can provide you with the necessary tools and emotional support to continue helping your loved one.

If you believe someone is in immediate danger, taking swift action is necessary.

1. **Stay with Them**: If possible, do not leave them alone. Your presence can provide comfort and reduce the risk of them acting on their thoughts. Stay calm and speak in a soothing manner.

2. **Contact Emergency Services**: If the situation becomes critical, call emergency services or take them

to the nearest emergency room. You can say, "I'm really worried about you and think we need to get some immediate help."

3. **Utilize Crisis Resources**: Familiarize yourself with crisis resources such as the Suicide & Crisis Lifeline (9-8-8) or Crisis Text Line (text "HELLO" to 741741) in the United States. These resources are available 24/7 and can provide immediate support and intervention. Every country has their own services, so find your nearest service and don't hesitate to use every facility at your disposal.

I remember moments when simple acts of kindness made a huge difference. A friend who sat with me in silence, just being there, provided immense comfort. Another time, someone asked me directly about my thoughts, and the relief of finally sharing my burden was truly what I needed. These moments of connection and understanding were lifelines that pulled me back from the brink.

Helping someone who may be suicidal is a daunting task, but it's also a benevolent act of compassion. You can make a significant difference by approaching the conversation with empathy, offering tangible support, understanding your limits, and knowing how to act in a crisis. Remember, you are not alone in this effort; professional help is available, and together, we can provide the support needed to navigate these dark times.

AFTERMATH OF SUICIDE ATTEMPTS

When the unimaginable happens and a loved one attempts suicide, the aftermath is often a messy and turbulent period filled with unstable emotions. The survivors; family, friends, and the individuals themselves, must follow a path through shock, guilt, anger, and sorrow. I have been on both sides of the curtain and it is a trial of personal resilience and strength on both ends of the straw. For healing and recovery, it is of utmost importance that we understand how to cope and support each other during this time.

In the immediate aftermath of a suicide attempt, emotions can be raw and overwhelming. Shock and disbelief are often the first reactions. It's a surreal experience to process that someone you care about has reached such a desperate point.

1. **Shock and Disbelief**: It's common to feel numb or detached initially. The mind struggles to process the gravity of what has occurred. When I was behind the curtain of the attempt, I felt unimaginable waves of guilt and shame. However, later in life, when I discovered that a friend had attempted suicide, I remember feeling like I was walking through a fog, the reality of the situation hitting me in waves of belief and disbelief.

2. **Guilt and Self-Blame**: Many people grapple with guilt and self-blame. They replay past interactions, searching for signs they might have missed or actions they could have taken. "What could I have done better?" is often an unavoidable question. This can be particularly intense for parents, siblings, spouse, or close friends. My family constantly wandered in this question, wondering if they had missed something in my behavior, blaming themselves for not preventing my attempt.

3. **Anger and Confusion**: Anger is another common reaction, both towards the person who attempted suicide and towards oneself or others. This can stem from feelings of helplessness and frustration. Confusion about why this happened and how it could have been prevented is also prevalent.

For the person who attempted suicide, the days and weeks following can be filled with a sense of vulnerability and fear. They may feel ashamed, embarrassed, or regretful, and these emotions need to be handled with utmost care and sensitivity.

1. **Providing a Safe Space**: Create a supportive and non-judgmental environment where they can express their feelings openly. Assure them that it's okay to talk about their emotions and experiences. I remember the relief I felt when my best friend simply sat with me, not pressing for answers but making it clear I wasn't alone.

2. **Encouraging Professional Help**: It's crucial to connect the survivor with mental health professionals who can provide the necessary support and treatment. This might include therapy, medication, or both. Helping them set up appointments and offering to accompany them can be very supportive.

3. **Reassuring and Reinforcing Their Value**: Reaffirming their worth and letting them know they are loved and valued is vital. This can help counteract feelings of worthlessness and despair. Simple affirmations like "You matter to me" or "I'm glad you're here" can make a significant difference.

4. **Monitoring and Safety Plans**: Implementing a safety plan can prevent future attempts. This includes removing access to means of self-harm, creating a list of emergency contacts, and establishing a support network. Frequent check-ins and monitoring their well-being are essential during this time.

Survivors of a loved one's suicide attempt often need support just as much as the person who attempted it. The emotional toll can be heavy, and knowing how to cope is important.

1. **Seeking Support Groups**: Joining support groups for families and friends of individuals who have attempted

suicide can provide a sense of community and understanding. Sharing experiences and coping strategies with others who have gone through similar situations can be incredibly comforting.

2. **Therapy for Loved Ones**: Family therapy can help address the emotional and relational impacts of a suicide attempt. It provides a platform to express feelings, resolve conflicts, and strengthen the family unit. Individual therapy can also be beneficial in processing personal emotions and developing coping mechanisms.

3. **Practicing Self-Care**: It's easy to become consumed with worry and care for the survivor, but it's equally important to take care of your own well-being. This includes maintaining a healthy lifestyle, getting enough rest, and engaging in activities that bring joy and relaxation. Self-care is not selfish; it's necessary to remain strong and supportive. As the airplane staff reminds us before every take off, *"put your oxygen mask on first, before helping others."*

4. **Understanding and Patience**: Healing takes time, and the road to recovery can be long and challenging. Patience and understanding are integral. Be prepared for setbacks and remain a constant source of support. Understanding that it's a journey, not a quick fix, can help manage expectations and maintain hope.

Moving forward after a suicide attempt involves rebuilding trust, developing open communication, and creating a supportive environment. It's a gradual process that requires dedication and resilience from everyone involved.

1. **Rebuilding Trust**: Trust might have been shaken, especially if there were feelings of betrayal or secrets involved. Open, honest communication can help rebuild

trust. Encourage the survivor to share their thoughts and feelings regularly, and do the same in return.

2. **Creating a Supportive Environment**: Make sure the survivor knows they are not alone. Regular family meetings, consistent check-ins, and fostering a positive, loving home environment can provide a sense of stability and safety.

3. **Celebrating Small Victories**: Recovery is a series of small steps forward. Celebrate the small victories, whether it's attending therapy sessions regularly, opening up more, or simply having a good day. Acknowledging progress can boost morale and reinforce the importance of the journey.

4. **Staying Informed**: Educate yourself about depression, suicide prevention, and mental health resources. Staying informed empowers you to better support your loved one and to recognize warning signs early.

In my life, the turning point wasn't a dramatic moment of realization but a series of small steps supported by those around me. Friends who reached out, family members who stayed patient, and therapists who guided me, all formed a part of my recovery. It was their unwavering support that helped me navigate the aftermath of my own suicide attempt.

The aftermath of a suicide attempt is a period of intense emotion and challenge, but it's also a time for healing and connection. We can help our loved ones, and ourselves, find a path to recovery by approaching the situation with empathy, providing unwavering support, and fostering open communication. Remember, you are not alone in this journey. Together, we can walk through the harsh realities of depression and suicide, lighting up hope and understanding every step of the way.

CONCLUDING PART 1

Depression is a complicated and dangerous condition that impacts every aspect of an individual's life. Throughout Part 1 of this book, we've dived into the depths of what depression is, how it manifests, and its profound effects on daily living, cognition, physical health, and relationships. This exploration is essential for both those suffering from depression and those around them to build a compassionate and informed approach to mental health.

As we have repeatedly emphasized, depression is not merely a state of prolonged sadness. It is an illness of genetic, biological, psychological, and environmental factors. Understanding these dimensions helps in recognizing that depression is not a sign of personal weakness but a significant mental health condition that requires empathy, support, and appropriate intervention.

From the biochemical imbalances involving neurotransmitters like serotonin, dopamine, and norepinephrine to the changes in brain structure and function, the biological underpinnings of depression reveal why it feels so inescapable. These biological factors are endorsed by psychological theories, such as the cognitive-behavioral models that highlight the significance of negative thought patterns and learned helplessness. Traumas, especially in early life, also leave indelible marks that contribute to the development and persistence of depression.

As we've explored, the impact of depression extends far beyond the mind, affecting the body and social interactions. The cognitive impairments, emotional numbness, chronic physical symptoms, and strained relationships form a web that entangles sufferers, often leading to increased isolation and despair. Recognizing these symptoms and their penetrative effects on daily functioning is essential for effective support and treatment. The link between depression and suicide is particularly harrowing, underscoring the importance of early recognition, intervention, and continuous support. Understanding the risk factors, warning signs, and intervention strategies can save lives and help those in crisis find a path toward recovery.

With a solid foundation of what depression is and its extensive impact, we now move into the second part of our journey: Managing Depression in Daily Life. Part 2 will provide practical strategies and insights for managing depression, focusing on coping mechanisms, treatment options, and pathways to recovery. There, we will explore various treatment modalities, from medication and psychotherapy to alternative therapies and lifestyle changes. We will understand these options to empower individuals for making informed decisions about their mental health care and find a personalized approach that works best for them.

We will also talk about the importance of building a support system, both personally and professionally. The role of family, friends, and community in supporting those with depression cannot be overstated. Creating a network of understanding and empathy is key to erecting a supportive environment conducive to healing.

Lastly, we will discuss the journey of recovery and resilience. Recovery is not a linear process but a path with its ups and downs. Embracing this journey with patience, hope, and self-compassion is essential. We aim to inspire and guide those struggling with depression toward a place of greater understanding, acceptance, and ultimately, resilience.

Let us carry forward the knowledge gained from understanding depression and proceed further with open hearts and minds, ready to explore the pathways of managing and overcoming depression. Together, we can find hope in the darkest of times, and work toward a brighter, more compassionate future.

PART 2: MANAGING DEPRESSION IN

DAILY LIFE

As we transition from understanding depression to managing it, we enter a phase of empowerment and action. While knowledge about depression's nature is important, learning how to tackle its challenges daily can transform lives. This part of the book is dedicated to equipping you with the tools, strategies, and insights necessary to manage depression effectively and reclaim a sense of normalcy and fulfillment.

When I first started dealing with my depression, I was overwhelmed by the sheer number of strategies and treatments available. It was like standing at the edge of a vast forest, unsure which path to take. Each trail promised a different method of coping or healing, from traditional medical treatments to holistic approaches. The journey can seem daunting, but my goal is to guide you through this forest, helping you find the paths that work best for you.

In **Chapter 5**, we will explore self-help techniques and daily management strategies. These are the small, everyday actions that can make a significant difference in how you feel. From establishing a routine to practicing mindfulness, these techniques are about taking control of your day-to-day life. They are the foundation upon which you can build a more stable and resilient mindset. When depression has you in its grip, even the smallest tasks can feel monumental. But by breaking your day into manageable chunks and focusing on achievable goals, you can start to regain a sense of control. I'll share some of the practices that helped me, like maintaining a daily journal, setting small, realistic goals, and finding moments of joy in simple activities.

While self-help techniques are vital, sometimes professional intervention is necessary. **Chapter 6** delves into the various professional treatments and therapies available for depression. We'll discuss the different types of psychotherapy, such as cognitive-behavioral therapy (CBT), Acceptance And Commitment Therapy (ACT), and psychodynamic therapy, and explore how these methods can help you understand and manage your depression. Similarly, medication is another important aspect of treatment for many people. Antidepressants can be significant in stabilizing mood and alleviating symptoms. We will cover the different classes of antidepressants, how they work, and what you can expect from them. Combining medication with therapy often provides the most effective treatment, creating a balanced approach to managing depression.

Chapter 7 focuses on lifestyle changes and coping strategies that can support your mental health journey. This includes everything from diet and exercise to sleep hygiene and social connections. Lifestyle changes can be powerful allies in the fight against depression. Regular physical activity, for instance, has been shown to boost mood and improve overall mental health. Diet is also involved here as nutrient-rich foods can help support brain health, while a balanced diet can stabilize your mood and energy levels. Sleep, often disrupted by depression, is another vital component of well-being. Establishing a healthy sleep routine can significantly improve your mental health. We'll also discuss the importance of building and maintaining a support network, as well as techniques for managing stress and anxiety.

Overall, part 2 of this book is about bridging the gap between understanding depression and taking actionable steps to manage it. It's about recognizing that while depression is a significant part of your life, it doesn't define you. With the right tools, strategies, and support, you can manage your symptoms and lead a fulfilling life. This journey is deeply personal, and what works for one person might not work for another. The key is to explore, experiment, and find the right combination of treatments and strategies that work for you. As we move through these chapters, remember that each step you take is a step towards regaining control and finding hope.

Depression can make you feel like you're lost in a dark tunnel with no way out. But there is a path forward, and together, we will find it. We'll explore various methods, from the well-established to the innovative, to help you manage your depression and reclaim your life.

Managing depression is a journey that extends beyond the therapist's office or the psychiatrist's prescription pad. It demands a holistic approach, integrating self-help techniques and daily management strategies that empower us to take control of our mental health. This chapter discusses the various self-help methods that can make a substantial difference in managing depression, bringing together practices that I have found invaluable in my own life.

Self-help techniques are not about replacing professional treatment but rather complementing it. They offer a sense of agency and empowerment, enabling you to actively participate in your own recovery. When depression makes you feel powerless, these techniques can help you reclaim some control.

One of the foundational self-help strategies is mindfulness and meditation. These practices involve focusing your mind on the present moment, acknowledging your thoughts and feelings without judgment. They can be powerful tools in reducing the symptoms of depression, helping you to break the cycle of negative thinking. Mindfulness and meditation offer a respite from the constant barrage of depressive thoughts, providing a space for peace and clarity.

Physical activity and diet must also be addressed for managing depression. Exercise is often referred to as nature's antidepressant, releasing endorphins that can boost your mood and energy levels. A well-balanced diet can provide the nutrients your brain needs to function optimally, supporting your overall mental health. The connection between the body and mind is profound, and nurturing your physical health can have a positive impact on your mental well-being.

Journaling and reflection are another powerful set of tools. Writing about your thoughts and feelings can provide a much-needed outlet for your emotions. It allows you to process your experiences, gain insights, and track your progress. Journaling can also help you identify patterns in your thoughts and behaviors, offering a clearer understanding of your depression and how to manage it.

Establishing daily routines and setting achievable goals are also critical components of self-help. Depression can make even the simplest tasks feel overwhelming, but having a structured routine can provide a sense of normalcy and predictability. Setting small, realistic goals can give you a sense of accomplishment and purpose, helping you to rebuild confidence and motivation.

I write about these self-help techniques because they have been invaluable in my own enlightenment. They are the small, daily practices that make a big difference over time. They have helped me to create a sense of stability and control in my life, providing the guidance to beat mental health challenges. These strategies are not quick fixes; they require time, patience, and consistency. But they are powerful allies in the fight against depression, offering a way to actively engage in your own healing process.

As we move through this chapter, we will explore each of these self-help techniques in detail. From mindfulness and meditation to physical activity and diet, journaling and reflection, and daily routines and goal setting, we will uncover how these practices can support your journey to managing depression. Each section will provide practical tips and insights, drawing from both personal experience and research, to help you integrate these techniques into your daily life.

Managing depression is a continuous process, and self-help techniques are an essential part of this journey. They offer a way to take proactive steps towards your mental health, empowering you to make positive changes and build resilience. Through these practices, you can find a path to healing and a way to deal with the complications of depression with greater ease and confidence.

Managing depression feels like battling an invisible foe. The mind races with negative thoughts, and the weight of sadness seems unbearable. During my darkest times, mindfulness and meditation became my sanctuary. These practices, rooted in ancient traditions and endorsed by modern psychology, offered a way to find calm amidst chaos. Once I learned that they are powerful tools for anyone grappling with depression, I used them to improve the overall quality of my mental health and to this day, advocate them as part of our everyday lives.

Mindfulness is the practice of being fully present in the moment, aware of where we are and what we're doing, without being overly reactive or overwhelmed by what's happening around us. Jon Kabat-Zinn, a pioneer in the field, defines it as *"paying attention in a particular way: on purpose, in the present moment, and non-judgmentally."* This simple yet awe-inspiring practice can be a lifeline for those struggling with depression.

In the book "The Mindful Way Through Depression," authors Mark Williams, John Teasdale, Zindel Segal, and Jon Kabat-Zinn explain how mindfulness can help break the cycle of chronic unhappiness. They describe mindfulness as a way to step out of automatic pilot mode and see our thoughts and feelings as transient states rather than reflections of absolute truth. This shift in perspective can be incredibly liberating.

Techniques of Mindfulness and Meditation

1. **Mindful Breathing:** One of the simplest and most effective mindfulness techniques is mindful breathing.

It involves focusing on the breath, observing each inhale and exhale without trying to change them. This practice helps anchor the mind, reducing the power of negative thoughts. When I first started, I used to set aside five minutes daily to sit quietly and focus on my breath. Slowly, this practice grew, and I found it easier to manage my racing thoughts. I now use mindful breathing as a consistent daily practice to keep myself grounded in the present.

2. **Body Scan Meditation:** Body scan meditation involves lying down and bringing attention to different parts of the body, from the toes to the head. This practice bridges a deeper connection with the body and helps identify areas of tension or discomfort. It's a powerful way to cultivate awareness and relax. During my depressive episodes, body scans helped me connect with my mind and body, reducing anxiety and promoting relaxation. It is also an amazing practice to battle insomnia.

3. **Loving-Kindness Meditation:** Loving-kindness meditation, or "*metta*," focuses on developing feelings of compassion and love towards oneself and others. It begins with sending loving-kindness to oneself, then gradually extending these feelings to loved ones, acquaintances, and even those with whom one has conflicts. This practice can be particularly helpful for those with depression, as it counters feelings of self-criticism and isolation. Incorporating loving-kindness meditation into my routine softened my inner dialogue and helped me cultivate a sense of connection and empathy by actively dealing with my inner critic.

4. **Mindful Walking:** Mindful walking is another accessible form of mindfulness practice. It involves paying attention to the sensation of walking, the movement of the legs, the feel of the ground beneath

the feet, and the rhythm of the breath. This practice combines the benefits of physical activity with mindfulness, making it doubly effective for managing depression. During particularly rough days, a short mindful walk in nature can provide a much-needed respite from spiraling thoughts.

The benefits of mindfulness and meditation are well-documented in both scientific literature and personal anecdotes. They offer numerous advantages for managing depression, like:

1. **Reduction in Symptoms:** Research has shown that mindfulness and meditation can significantly reduce symptoms of depression. A study published in JAMA Internal Medicine found that mindfulness meditation can help alleviate symptoms of depression, anxiety, and pain. Through mindfulness, individuals can learn to observe their thoughts and feelings without judgment, reducing the impact of negative emotions.

2. **Improved Emotional Regulation:** Mindfulness helps improve emotional regulation, allowing individuals to respond to emotional triggers with greater equanimity. This is particularly beneficial for those with depression, who often experience heightened emotional reactivity. Through mindfulness, I learned to observe my emotions without getting swept away by them, which was an essential step in managing my depression.

3. **Enhanced Self-Awareness:** Practicing mindfulness increases self-awareness, helping individuals recognize patterns in their thoughts and behaviors. This heightened awareness can lead to more informed decisions and healthier coping mechanisms. For me, mindfulness illuminated the connection between my thoughts and moods, enabling me to intervene before spiraling into deeper depression.

4. **Increased Resilience:** Mindfulness builds resilience by promoting a non-judgmental attitude towards oneself and one's experiences. It encourages acceptance and self-compassion, which are essential for overcoming the challenges of depression. Over time, I found that mindfulness practice made me more resilient, better able to withstand the ups and downs of life.

5. **Physical Health Benefits:** The mind-body connection means that improving mental health can also enhance physical health. Mindfulness and meditation have been linked to reduced blood pressure, improved sleep, and decreased inflammation. These physical health benefits complement the mental health advantages, creating a holistic approach to managing depression.

Integrating mindfulness into daily life doesn't require long meditation sessions. It can be as simple as taking a few moments throughout the day to pause, breathe, and observe. Mindful eating, mindful listening, and even mindful chores can transform routine activities into opportunities for presence and awareness. For instance, while washing dishes, focus on the sensation of the water, the texture of the soap bubbles, and the act of cleaning each dish. This simple shift in attention can turn a mundane task into a meditative practice. Similarly, practicing mindfulness during conversations can improve communication and deepen connections with others.

Incorporating mindfulness and meditation into my daily routine has been transformative. It hasn't been a magic cure, but it has provided a steady foundation on which I can build healthier habits and coping strategies. The journey with mindfulness is ongoing, and each day presents new opportunities to practice and grow. Through mindfulness, I've learned to approach my thoughts and feelings with curiosity rather than judgment. I've discovered the power of the present moment and found solace in the simple act of breathing. These practices have not only helped manage my depression but also enriched my overall quality of life.

As we move forward in this chapter, we will explore other self-help techniques that can complement mindfulness and meditation. Each of these methods offers unique benefits and can be tailored to fit individual needs. Together, they form a comprehensive toolkit for managing depression and enhancing well-being.

PHYSICAL ACTIVITY AND DIET

Physical activity is one of the most surprising lifelines in the throes of our darkest days. Exercise, which I once viewed as a chore, is an important part of the healing journey toward mental wellness. Alongside this, reevaluating your diet is also involved in managing depression. It turns out that the old adage *"you are what you eat"* holds more truth than I initially realized, particularly when it comes to mental health.

Physical Activity and Mental Health

Physical activity and mental health are intrinsically linked. Exercise has been shown to have formidable effects on brain function and mental well-being. When you engage in physical activity, your brain releases chemicals such as endorphins and serotonin, which act as natural mood lifters. These chemicals help reduce the perception of pain and trigger positive feelings, much like the effects of antidepressants. This is particularly relevant for those with depression, as these neurotransmitters are often imbalanced. Regular physical activity helps to restore their levels, providing a natural boost to mood and overall mental health. For example, when I started incorporating regular walks into my routine, I noticed a marked improvement in my mood. Even on days when leaving the house felt like an impossible task, the effort paid off. The rhythm of walking, the fresh air, and the sense of accomplishment created a cocktail of benefits that gradually lifted my spirits.

Physical activity also reduces levels of the body's stress hormones, such as adrenaline and cortisol. Lowering these hormones can alleviate anxiety and reduce stress. Engaging in exercises like yoga or tai chi, which emphasize mindful movement and breath control, can be particularly beneficial. These practices not only promote physical health but also cultivate a state of mental calm and focus. When I felt overwhelmed by anxiety, yoga became my refuge. The gentle stretching, combined with deep breathing exercises, helped release physical tension and clear my mind. It was a form of moving meditation that brought me back to the present moment, away from the spiraling thoughts of depression.

Regular exercise helps build resilience by improving self-esteem and body image. The sense of accomplishment from meeting fitness goals, no matter how small, can boost confidence and provide a sense of control over one's life. This empowerment can be particularly healing for someone battling depression, where feelings of helplessness and worthlessness are common. I remember the first time I ran a mile without stopping. It seemed like a small victory, but it was monumental for me. It was a tangible achievement that I could hold onto, a reminder that I was capable of more than I believed. These small wins accumulated, gradually rebuilding my confidence and resilience.

Diet and Mental Health

Just as exercise can influence mental health, so too can diet. What we eat directly affects our brain function and, consequently, our mood and mental health. Nutrient-rich foods provide the building blocks for neurotransmitters and support overall brain health.

The gut and brain are connected through the gut-brain axis, a communication network linking the emotional and cognitive centers of the brain with peripheral intestinal functions. The gut microbiome, the community of microorganisms living in our intestines, is a critical contributor in this interaction. A healthy gut microbiome can positively influence mood and cognitive function, while an imbalanced microbiome has been linked to depression and anxiety. Eating a diet rich in fruits, vegetables, whole grains, lean proteins, and fermented foods can promote a healthy gut microbiome. Foods like yogurt, sauerkraut, and kimchi are excellent sources of probiotics, which support gut health. When you start paying attention to your diet, incorporating more of these nutrient-dense foods, you will notice a significant improvement in your overall mood and energy levels.

Certain nutrients are particularly beneficial for mental health. Omega-3 fatty acids, found in fatty fish like salmon and mackerel, are known for their anti-inflammatory properties and ability to support brain function. Studies have shown that omega-3s can help reduce symptoms of depression and anxiety. Similarly, B vitamins, especially B12 and folate, are critical for brain health and the production of neurotransmitters. Leafy greens, legumes, nuts, and seeds are excellent sources of these vitamins. Iron, zinc, and magnesium also pitch in for maintaining mental health. Ensuring an adequate intake of these nutrients can help mitigate the symptoms of depression.

On the flip side, certain foods and substances can exacerbate depression. Highly processed foods, high in sugar and unhealthy fats, can lead to inflammation and negatively impact brain function. Limiting the intake of these foods, along with caffeine and alcohol, can help stabilize mood and energy levels. I have personally noticed the stark difference when I cut back on sugar and processed foods. My energy levels become more stable, and I experience fewer mood swings. This isn't an overnight transformation, but gradually, these dietary changes contribute to a more balanced and resilient mental state.

Integrating Exercise and Healthy Eating into Daily Life

Incorporating regular physical activity and a balanced diet into daily life doesn't have to be overwhelming. Start small, with manageable changes that can be sustained over time. Here are some practical tips:

1. Start with Small, Achievable Goals: Setting small, realistic goals can make the process less daunting. Begin with short walks, a few minutes of stretching, or a single healthy meal each day. Celebrate these small victories to build momentum and motivation.

2. Find Activities You Enjoy: Choose physical activities that you enjoy and that fit your lifestyle. Whether it's dancing, swimming, hiking, or playing a sport, finding joy in movement can make exercise feel less like a chore and more like a rewarding part of your day.

3. Plan and Prepare Meals: Meal planning and preparation can help ensure you have healthy options available, reducing the temptation to opt for less nutritious convenience foods. Batch cooking, healthy snacks, and easy-to-make recipes can simplify the process.

4. Seek Support and Accountability: Having a support system can make a significant difference. Share your goals with friends or family, join a fitness class, or find an online community. Accountability and encouragement from others can help keep you on track.

5. Be Kind to Yourself: Remember that progress isn't linear. There will be days when it's harder to stick to your routines, and that's okay. Be gentle with yourself and recognize that each day is a new opportunity to take small steps towards better mental health.

Incorporating physical activity and a healthy diet into your life can be transformative. These practices not only support physical health but also provide powerful tools for managing depression. As we continue exploring self-help techniques, we'll look at other strategies that can complement these practices and further enhance well-being.

JOURNALING AND REFLECTION

When depression grips you, it can feel like a never-ending cycle of negative thoughts and emotions. One powerful way to break this cycle is through journaling and reflection. Writing has always been a therapeutic tool for me, and over time, I've discovered how putting pen to paper can help untangle the complex web of thoughts and emotions that depression weaves.

Writing has a unique ability to help us process and understand our experiences. It provides a safe space to explore our thoughts and feelings without judgment. When I started journaling, it felt like opening a pressure valve, releasing pent-up emotions that I struggled to articulate verbally. Writing can serve as a form of self-therapy, allowing us to gain clarity and insight into our mental state.

1. Emotional Release: One of the most immediate benefits of journaling is emotional release. The act of writing down your feelings can be incredibly cathartic. It's a way to pour out everything that's been festering inside, giving those emotions a voice. Imagine the relief of finally expressing anger, sadness, or frustration that you've been holding in. Journaling allows these feelings to be acknowledged and validated, which is a crucial step in the healing process. For instance, during my darkest times, I found solace in writing letters to my depression. I would address it directly, pouring out my grievances and frustrations. These letters were never meant to be read by anyone else; they were a way for me to confront and externalize my internal struggles. Each word felt like a small weight lifted from my shoulders.

2. Identifying Patterns and Triggers: Journaling can also help identify patterns and triggers in your thoughts and behaviors. By regularly documenting your experiences, you may begin to notice recurring themes or situations that exacerbate your depression. This awareness is the first step towards change. Consider keeping a mood journal where you track your daily emotions, activities, and thoughts. Over time, you might see patterns emerge, such as feeling particularly low after certain events or interactions. This insight can be invaluable in understanding your depression and finding ways to manage it.

3. Cognitive Restructuring: Cognitive-behavioral therapy (CBT) often involves examining and challenging negative thought patterns. Journaling can complement this process by providing a tangible way to explore and reframe your thoughts. When you write about a negative experience, you can also challenge the underlying assumptions and beliefs that contribute to your depression. For example, if you write about a situation where you felt like a failure, you can take the opportunity to question that perception. Was it really a failure, or are you being too hard on yourself? What did you learn from the experience? This kind of reflective writing can help shift your mindset from one of self-criticism to one of self-compassion and growth.

4. Setting Intentions and Goals: Journaling is not just about looking back; it's also about looking forward. Setting intentions and goals through writing can provide direction and motivation. It gives you a sense of purpose and control over your life, which is often diminished in depression. Every morning, I started writing down three intentions for the day. These were simple, achievable goals like "take a walk," "call a friend," or "read a chapter of a book." Writing these intentions helped me focus on positive actions and gave me small victories to celebrate, no matter how minor they seemed.

Techniques for Effective Journaling

To get the most out of journaling, it helps to have some techniques and prompts to guide you. Here are a few strategies that have been particularly effective for me:

1. Free Writing: Free writing is a technique where you write continuously for a set period without worrying about grammar, spelling, or punctuation. The goal is to keep the pen moving and let your thoughts flow freely. This can help bypass your internal criticism and access deeper, unfiltered emotions. Set a timer for 10 to 15 minutes and start writing whatever comes to mind. Don't stop to think or edit; just let the words spill out. This practice can reveal surprising insights and help release emotions you didn't even realize you were holding onto.

2. Guided Prompts: Sometimes, starting with a blank page can be intimidating. Guided prompts can provide a helpful starting point. Here are a few prompts to get you started:

- What are three things you are grateful for today?
- Describe a recent challenge and how you handled it.
- Write a letter to your younger self.
- What does your ideal day look like?

Using prompts can help focus your writing and explore specific aspects of your life and emotions.

3. Reflective Journaling: Reflective journaling involves looking back on past experiences and reflecting on what you've learned. This can be particularly useful for understanding how you've grown and changed over time. It also provides an opportunity to celebrate your progress, no matter how small. Take some time each week to review your journal entries. Reflect on what you've written and consider how your thoughts and feelings have evolved. This practice can provide valuable insights and reinforce your growth and resilience.

4. Artistic Journaling: If you're creatively inclined, incorporating art into your journaling can be a powerful tool. Drawing, painting, or collaging can provide an additional layer of expression. Sometimes, visual representation can convey emotions that words cannot. During particularly tough times, I would doodle or sketch alongside my journal entries. These images often captured my feelings more vividly than words alone. Artistic journaling allowed me to express myself in a different medium and provided a therapeutic outlet for my emotions.

Journaling has been a constant companion in my journey with depression. It has provided a safe space to explore my thoughts, release my emotions, and track my progress. There were days when writing felt like a lifeline, a way to anchor myself amid the storm. Through journaling, I learned to listen to my inner voice and understand my own needs and feelings. It helped me recognize patterns in my behavior and thought processes, giving me the tools to challenge and change them. Writing also gave me a sense of agency, a way to reclaim control over my life.

One of the most memorable moments in my journaling journey was when I stumbled upon an old entry from a particularly dark period. Reading my own words, I was struck by the depth of my despair at that time. But I was also able to see how far I had come since then. It was a powerful reminder of my resilience and the progress I had made.

Incorporating Journaling into Daily Life

To make journaling a regular part of your life, it helps to establish a routine. Set aside a specific time each day, whether it's in the morning to set intentions or in the evening to reflect on your day. Create a comfortable and inviting space for your writing practice, free from distractions. Remember, there are no rules in journaling. It's a personal practice, and it's important to find what works best for you. Whether you write a few lines or several pages, the key is consistency and honesty. Allow yourself to be vulnerable and authentic in your writing.

Journaling is a powerful tool for managing depression. It provides a space for emotional release, self-reflection, and personal growth. By incorporating journaling into your daily life, you can gain valuable insights, track your progress, and build resilience. As we continue to explore self-help techniques, we'll look at other strategies that can complement these practices and further enhance well-being.

Daily Routines and Goal Setting

The sheer thought of establishing a daily routine or setting goals can seem overwhelming when you're living with depression. I remember days when just getting out of bed felt like climbing a mountain. However, creating structure and setting achievable goals are powerful tools in managing depression. They provide a sense of purpose and accomplishment, no matter how small the steps might seem.

Daily routines offer a framework that can bring stability to the chaotic experience of depression. When you're depressed, unpredictability and a lack of structure can exacerbate feelings of helplessness and anxiety. Establishing a routine helps to create a predictable environment, which can reduce stress and provide a sense of control.

1. Building a Morning Routine: Mornings can set the tone for the rest of the day. Crafting a simple, manageable morning routine can make a significant difference. Start with small, achievable tasks that signal the beginning of the day. This might include making your bed, having a cup of tea or coffee, and getting dressed. The key is consistency. Even on days when depression feels most overwhelming, sticking to these small tasks can provide a sense of normalcy and accomplishment. For instance, my morning routine starts with a few minutes of deep breathing exercises, followed by a healthy breakfast. These small actions help ground me and prepare me for the day ahead. I've found that beginning the day with a bit of self-care sets a positive tone and helps mitigate some of the heaviness of depression. In fact, even when I am late for work, I try not to skip these habits because I firmly believe in "*mind over matter.*"

2. Structuring the Day: Beyond the morning, structuring your day with regular activities can help maintain momentum. Break your day into manageable chunks and include activities that promote well-being. This might involve scheduling time for exercise, meal preparation, work or study, and leisure activities. Creating a daily schedule might seem daunting at first, but start simple. Use a planner or an app to map out your day, even if it's just noting down meal times and breaks. Having a visual representation of your day can make it feel more manageable and less overwhelming.

3. Evening Routine: An evening routine can help signal the end of the day and prepare your mind for rest. Establishing calming activities before bed, such as reading, listening to music, or taking a warm bath, can improve sleep quality, which is often disrupted in depression. Avoiding screens and engaging in relaxing activities can help transition from the day's stresses to a restful night. This might be easier said than done, but remember what's at stake and maybe your despair will drive you to take these positive self-care steps.

Setting Achievable Goals

Setting goals can provide direction and motivation, but it's important to keep them realistic and achievable, especially when managing depression. Goals should be small, specific, and attainable, building a sense of accomplishment and progress over time.

1. Start Small: Begin with small, daily goals that are easy to achieve. These might include tasks like tidying a small area of your room, taking a short walk, or spending a few minutes on a hobby. These small victories can build confidence and momentum, creating a positive feedback loop. I encourage setting the goal of going for a five-minute walk each day. Initially, it might feel like a monumental task, but accomplishing it will give you a sense of achievement. Over time, you will be able to gradually increase the duration of these walks, and with it, your confidence will grow, leading to a positive feedback loop.

2. Use the SMART Framework: The SMART framework (Specific, Measurable, Achievable, Relevant, Time-bound) is a useful tool for setting goals. Ensure your goals are clear and specific, measurable so you can track progress, achievable given your current situation, relevant to your overall well-being, and time-bound to give a sense of urgency and focus. For example, instead of setting a vague goal like "exercise more," a SMART goal would be, "Walk for 15 minutes three times a week." This goal is specific, measurable, and time-bound, making it easier to track and achieve.

3. Celebrate Progress: Recognizing and celebrating progress, no matter how small, is essential. Depression often clouds our perception, making it difficult to see achievements. Keeping a journal to record your daily accomplishments can serve as a reminder of your progress. For instance, after completing a goal, reward yourself with something enjoyable, like watching a favorite show, enjoying a treat, or spending time on a hobby. These rewards can reinforce positive behavior and provide motivation to continue setting and achieving goals.

4. Be Flexible: While routines and goals are helpful, it's also important to be flexible. Depression can be unpredictable, and there will be days when sticking to a routine or achieving goals feels impossible. Allow yourself grace and adjust your plans as needed. The aim is progress, not perfection. If a particular goal feels too challenging on a given day, modify it to make it more attainable. For example, if the goal was to clean the entire kitchen but that feels overwhelming, focus on cleaning just one section. Flexibility ensures that you can adapt to your current state without feeling like you've failed.

Establishing routines and setting goals has been a cornerstone of my own journey with depression. These practices provided structure and a sense of purpose during times when I felt lost. The small, consistent actions built up over time, leading to significant improvements in my mental health. One of the most impactful changes I made was integrating mindfulness into my daily routine. By setting aside just a few minutes each day for meditation, I found a way to center myself and reduce anxiety. This small practice became a vital part of my daily routine, helping me navigate the ups and downs of depression. Setting goals, no matter how small, gave me something to strive for. They provided a sense of direction and purpose, which is often missing in depression. Each goal achieved, whether it was taking a walk or completing a task, reinforced my ability to make positive changes in my life.

To incorporate routines and goal setting into your daily life, start with small, manageable changes. Identify areas where you can create consistency and set achievable goals that align with your well-being. Remember to be patient and kind to yourself, recognizing that progress is gradual. Create a daily planner or use a digital app to map out your routine and track your goals. Having a visual representation can make it easier to stay on track and celebrate your progress.

Routines and goal setting are powerful tools in managing depression. They provide structure, purpose, and a sense of accomplishment, helping to counteract the chaos and helplessness that often accompany the condition. By incorporating these practices into your daily life, you can build resilience and foster a greater sense of control over your mental health. As we continue to explore self-help techniques, we'll go into professional treatments and therapies that complement these strategies and offer additional support.

KEY TAKEAWAYS

Living with depression is an arduous journey, one that can feel overwhelmingly isolating and exhausting. However, as we've explored in this chapter, incorporating self-help techniques into your daily routine can significantly improve your mental health and overall well-being. These practices are not quick fixes but rather tools that, when used consistently, can foster resilience and a sense of control over your life.

Mindfulness and meditation offer a sanctuary from the relentless negative thoughts that accompany depression. By focusing on the present moment and cultivating awareness, you can create a mental space where you are not defined by your depression. Starting with just a few minutes a day, these practices can gradually expand, providing a consistent source of calm and clarity. For instance, consider setting aside five minutes each morning to sit quietly and focus on your breath. Over time, you might find that this small practice becomes a cornerstone of your daily routine, offering a much-needed pause in the chaos. Apps like Headspace or Calm can provide guided meditations to help you get started.

Simultaneously, the benefits of physical activity and a balanced diet cannot be overstated. Regular exercise releases endorphins, which act as natural mood lifters. Even a short walk around your neighborhood can make a difference. Pairing physical activity with a diet rich in nutrients supports both physical and mental health, offering a foundation upon which you can build stronger resilience against depression. You don't need to become a fitness fanatic overnight. Start with manageable goals like walking for 10 minutes each day or incorporating more fruits and vegetables into your meals. The key is consistency and gradual progress. Over time, these small changes can lead to significant improvements in how you feel.

Further, journaling provides a safe space to explore and process your thoughts and emotions. It's a private dialogue with yourself that can reveal patterns, triggers, and insights into your mental health. By dedicating a few minutes each day to writing, you can gain clarity and perspective, which are crucial for managing depression. Consider starting a gratitude journal, where you note down things you're thankful for each day. This practice can shift your focus from what's going wrong to what's going right, nourishing a more positive outlook. Reflecting on your journey through writing can also be empowering, reminding you of your strength and progress.

Routines and goals provide structure and purpose, essential elements for managing depression. Establishing a daily routine can create a sense of normalcy and predictability, reducing anxiety and stress. Setting small, achievable goals can provide a sense of accomplishment and progress, which are paramount for maintaining motivation and self-esteem. Start with simple routines, like a morning ritual of stretching and breakfast or an evening wind-down routine involving reading or listening to calming music. When setting goals, ensure they are realistic and attainable. Celebrate your successes, no matter how small, and be kind to yourself if you encounter setbacks.

Integrating these self-help techniques into your daily life requires patience and persistence. It's important to remember that progress is gradual and that each small step forward is a victory. You are not alone in this journey. Many have walked this path and found light at the end of the tunnel through consistent practice of these strategies.

Encourage yourself to try different techniques and find what works best for you. Some days will be harder than others, but the cumulative effect of these practices can lead to significant improvements in your mental health. Reach out for support when needed, and don't hesitate to seek professional help if you find these self-help strategies alone are not enough.

As you continue on your journey, remember that these techniques are tools to help you manage depression, not cure it. They provide a way to cope, to find moments of peace and clarity amidst the struggle. You can create a supportive framework that enhances your resilience and fosters a more positive outlook on life by incorporating mindfulness, physical activity, journaling, and structured routines into your daily life. In the next chapter, we will delve into professional treatments and therapies that can complement these self-help techniques, providing a more comprehensive approach to managing depression.

To manage depression, professional treatments and therapies serve as essential guides with structured paths out of the maze. While self-help techniques can be incredibly beneficial, they are often most effective when combined with professional support. This chapter discusses the various professional treatment options available, providing a comprehensive overview to help you navigate the choices and find what works best for you. Professional treatment for depression encompasses a broad spectrum, from traditional psychotherapy and medications to emerging therapies that harness the latest advancements in neuroscience. Understanding these options is extremely important, as depression manifests uniquely in each individual. What works wonders for one person may not be as effective for another, making a personalized approach essential.

Psychotherapy, often referred to as *"talk therapy,"* is a cornerstone in the treatment of depression. It involves working with a trained therapist to explore the underlying issues contributing to depression, develop coping strategies, and develop healthier thinking patterns. Various forms of psychotherapy have been developed to address different aspects of depression, each with its unique methodology and focus.

Cognitive Behavioral Therapy (CBT) is one of the most widely researched and effective forms of therapy for depression. It focuses on identifying and challenging negative thought patterns and behaviors that contribute to depressive symptoms. Acceptance and Commitment Therapy (ACT) is another approach that encourages individuals to accept their thoughts and feelings rather than fighting or feeling guilty about them, and to commit to actions that align with their values. Psychodynamic therapy dives deeper into an individual's past experiences and emotional development, aiming to uncover and address unresolved conflicts that may be influencing current behavior.

Medications can vitally contribute in managing depression, particularly for those with moderate to severe symptoms. Antidepressants work by balancing the chemicals in the brain that affect mood and emotions. There are several types of antidepressants, each functioning differently and suited to different needs. Selective Serotonin Reuptake Inhibitors (SSRIs) are the most commonly prescribed antidepressants, known for their effectiveness and relatively mild side effects. Serotonin-Norepinephrine Reuptake Inhibitors (SNRIs) and Tricyclic Antidepressants (TCAs) are other options, each with its own mechanism and potential benefits. As it often involves some trial and error under the guidance of a healthcare provider, understanding the potential side effects and the process of finding the right medication is imperative.

The options for the treatment of depression are continually evolving, with emerging therapies offering new hope for those who have not found relief through traditional methods. Treatments such as ketamine infusions and psychedelic-assisted therapy are gaining attention for their rapid and profound effects on depression symptoms. These therapies work differently from traditional antidepressants, often targeting brain pathways that have been previously overlooked. Combining various treatments can often yield the best results. A multidisciplinary approach, which includes psychotherapy, medication, lifestyle changes, and emerging treatments, can address the multifaceted nature of depression more effectively than any single method. This approach allows for a more comprehensive treatment plan that is tailored to an individual's specific needs, ensuring a holistic path to recovery.

The goal of professional treatment is not just to alleviate symptoms but to provide individuals with the tools and strategies they need to manage their depression in the long term. Regular sessions with a therapist, consistent medication management, and openness to new and emerging treatments can create a solid foundation for recovery. Individuals can build resilience, develop healthier coping mechanisms, and ultimately reclaim control over their mental health by integrating these professional treatments into daily life.

As we dive into this chapter, we will explore each of these treatment options in detail, offering insights into their processes, benefits, and potential challenges. Whether you are just beginning your journey with depression treatment or looking for additional strategies to enhance your current approach, this chapter aims to provide the knowledge and guidance you need to make informed decisions about your mental health care.

PSYCHOTHERAPY

When I first walked into a therapist's office, I was uncertain and wary. The idea of sitting across from a stranger, divulging my deepest fears and insecurities, felt daunting. But as I progressed through therapy, I discovered its immeasurable impact. Psychotherapy isn't just a series of conversations; it's a structured approach designed to help individuals understand and navigate their mental health challenges. Let's explore some of the most effective types of therapy for treating depression.

Cognitive Behavioral Therapy (CBT)

CBT is often considered the gold standard in depression treatment. Developed by Aaron Beck in the 1960s, CBT is grounded in the idea that our thoughts, feelings, and behaviors are interconnected. Negative thought patterns can trap us in a cycle of depression, and by identifying and challenging these thoughts, we can alter our emotional and behavioral responses.

In my own experience, CBT helped me recognize the cognitive distortions that fueled my depression. Thoughts like "I'm a failure" or "Nothing will ever get better" were automatic and relentless. CBT taught me to question these thoughts and replace them with more balanced, realistic ones. For instance, instead of thinking "I'm a failure," I learned to say, "I've faced setbacks, but that doesn't define my worth." This shift in thinking was empowering and transformative.

CBT typically involves structured sessions with specific goals. Techniques like cognitive restructuring, behavioral activation, and exposure therapy are commonly used. Cognitive restructuring helps individuals identify and change negative thought patterns, while behavioral activation encourages engagement in activities that bring joy and satisfaction. Exposure therapy, often used for anxiety disorders, can also be beneficial for depression, helping individuals confront and reduce their fears.

Acceptance and Commitment Therapy (ACT)

Unlike CBT, which focuses on changing negative thoughts, ACT encourages individuals to accept their thoughts and feelings without judgment. The core idea is that struggling against negative thoughts can sometimes exacerbate them. Instead, ACT promotes psychological flexibility – the ability to stay present and engaged in life despite emotional pain.

I found ACT particularly helpful during times when my depressive thoughts were overwhelming. Instead of trying to fight these thoughts, ACT taught me to acknowledge them and let them pass without letting them control my actions. Techniques like mindfulness and values-based action are central to ACT. Mindfulness helps individuals stay grounded in the present moment, while values-based action encourages living in alignment with one's core values, even in the face of depression. For example, during a particularly tough period, I practiced mindfulness to stay connected to the present, focusing on my breath and the sensations around me. Simultaneously, I committed to small actions aligned with my values, like spending time with loved ones and engaging in creative pursuits. These practices didn't eliminate my depression, but they helped me navigate it with greater resilience.

Psychodynamic Therapy

Psychodynamic therapy, rooted in the theories of Freud, Jung, and other early psychoanalysts, takes a different approach. It focuses on uncovering unconscious processes and unresolved conflicts from the past that influence present behavior. The goal is to gain insight into these underlying issues, fostering emotional growth and symptom relief.

In my therapy journey, psychodynamic techniques helped me explore how early experiences and relationships shaped my self-perception and coping mechanisms. For instance, reflecting on my childhood and family dynamics revealed patterns of perfectionism and self-criticism that contributed to my depression. Understanding these patterns allowed me to address them more effectively.

Psychodynamic therapy often involves exploring dreams, free association, and examining the therapeutic relationship itself. It requires a willingness to delve deep into one's psyche and can be a longer-term process compared to CBT or ACT. However, for many, including myself, the insights gained through psychodynamic therapy can be deeply healing.

While each of these therapies offers unique benefits, many therapists integrate elements from different approaches to tailor treatment to individual needs. This integrative approach recognizes that depression is multifaceted, and a one-size-fits-all method may not be sufficient. For example, my therapy journey included elements of CBT, ACT, and psychodynamic therapy. During different phases of my depression, different techniques were more or less effective. Initially, CBT provided the structure and skills needed to challenge my negative thoughts. As I progressed, ACT's mindfulness practices helped me stay present and engaged. Finally, psychodynamic exploration offered deeper insights into my emotional patterns and relationships.

Effectiveness and Accessibility

The effectiveness of these therapies is well-supported by research. Numerous studies have shown that CBT is highly effective for depression, often producing significant improvements in symptoms within a few months. ACT has also gained empirical support, particularly for its ability to enhance psychological flexibility and reduce depressive symptoms. Psychodynamic therapy, while less extensively studied, has shown effectiveness, especially for those with complex or long-standing depression. However, accessibility remains a challenge. Finding a qualified therapist, affording sessions, and committing to regular appointments can be daunting. Online therapy platforms and community mental health services can help bridge this gap, making therapy more accessible to those in need.

As we move forward in this chapter, we'll explore other professional treatments, including medications and emerging therapies. Each treatment option offers its own pathway to healing, and understanding these options empowers us to make informed choices on our journey toward mental wellness. Exploring these therapies is a step toward understanding that managing depression often requires a multifaceted approach. Each type of therapy offers a unique lens through which to view and address depression. Whether it's the structured approach of CBT, the acceptance-based techniques of ACT, or the deep exploration of psychodynamic therapy, there is a wealth of strategies available to help navigate the complexities of depression.

MEDICATIONS

I have known so many people throughout my life, whom I could see struggling with mental health issues but never considered seeking professional help or medication. "I will be labeled crazy," they said. I've seen the harm that the social stigma around mental health medication can cause and it's painful to watch. When I first considered medication for my depression, I was filled with uncertainty and fear. The idea of altering my brain chemistry felt both foreign and intimidating.

Yet, as I dove deeper into understanding antidepressants, I realized their potential to provide relief and stability. Medication can be a huge factor in managing depression, often working in tandem with therapy to create a comprehensive treatment plan. Let's explore the common types of antidepressants, their benefits, and the potential side effects so the next time you encounter them, you have a basic understanding of what they are. This section isn't meant for self-medication but rather to educate you about the basic classes of medicines that you may come across, when getting professional help or dealing with someone who is taking these medicines.

Selective Serotonin Reuptake Inhibitors (SSRIs)

SSRIs are often the first line of defense in the pharmacological treatment of depression. SSRIs work by increasing the levels of serotonin in the brain, a neurotransmitter that plays a key role in mood regulation. Common SSRIs include fluoxetine (Prozac), sertraline (Zoloft), and escitalopram (Lexapro). The benefits of SSRIs are well-documented. For many, these medications can significantly reduce symptoms of depression, making daily life more manageable. They tend to have fewer side effects compared to older classes of antidepressants, which makes them a popular choice. I no longer remember when I started my pharmacological journey, but I remember that within a few weeks, I felt a noticeable lift in my mood. It wasn't a miraculous transformation, but the dark cloud that had been looming over me seemed a little less heavy.

However, SSRIs are not without their side effects. Common issues include nausea, headaches, and sexual dysfunction. Some individuals experience increased anxiety or insomnia when they first start taking SSRIs. It's important to have an open dialogue with your doctor about these side effects, as they can often be managed or may diminish over time. In my case, the weight fluctuations and nausea were challenging, but after adjusting the dosages, my body gradually adapted and started exhibiting positive results.

Serotonin and Norepinephrine Reuptake Inhibitors (SNRIs)

SNRIs are another class of antidepressants. They work by increasing the levels of both serotonin and norepinephrine in the brain. Common SNRIs include venlafaxine (Effexor) and duloxetine (Cymbalta). SNRIs can be particularly effective for individuals who do not respond adequately to SSRIs. They not only address the mood symptoms of depression but can also be helpful for chronic pain, which is often comorbid with depression. For example, duloxetine is frequently prescribed to manage both depression and pain associated with conditions like fibromyalgia. The side effects of SNRIs are similar to those of SSRIs, including nausea, dizziness, and sexual dysfunction. Additionally, SNRIs can sometimes increase blood pressure, so regular monitoring is essential. Imagine, if someone switches from an SSRI to an SNRI due to persistent pain issues; the transition may come with some initial side effects like dizziness, but the dual benefits of mood and pain improvement might make a significant difference in their quality of life.

Tricyclic Antidepressants (TCAs)

TCAs are one of the older classes of antidepressants. They work by affecting a range of neurotransmitters, including serotonin and norepinephrine. Common TCAs include amitriptyline and nortriptyline. While TCAs can be highly effective, especially in cases of severe depression, they are often not the first choice due to their side effect profile. TCAs can cause dry mouth, blurred vision, constipation, and urinary retention. They also carry a risk of cardiovascular side effects, which necessitates careful monitoring, particularly in individuals with pre-existing heart conditions. Despite their drawbacks, TCAs can be lifesaving for individuals who do not respond to other medications. I have personally known people who relied on TCAs when other medications had failed. According to them, the side effects were challenging, but with careful management, they found significant relief from depressive symptoms.

Monoamine Oxidase Inhibitors (MAOIs)

MAOIs are another older class of antidepressants. They work by inhibiting the action of monoamine oxidase, an enzyme that breaks down neurotransmitters like serotonin, norepinephrine, and dopamine. Common MAOIs include phenelzine (Nardil) and tranylcypromine (Parnate).

MAOIs can be very effective for certain types of depression, particularly atypical depression. However, they require strict dietary restrictions to avoid potentially dangerous interactions with tyramine, a substance found in certain foods and drinks. This can be a significant lifestyle adjustment, making MAOIs less convenient than other options. Additionally, MAOIs can interact with other medications, so it's crucial to manage these prescriptions carefully. There are numerous occasions where people who were prescribed MAOI as a last resort after they had tried every other class of antidepressant without success. The dietary restrictions are cumbersome, but the improvement in mood and overall functioning was noticeable, highlighting the potential benefits of these powerful medications.

Atypical Antidepressants

Atypical antidepressants do not fit neatly into the other categories and include medications like bupropion (Wellbutrin) and mirtazapine (Remeron). Bupropion works primarily on the neurotransmitters dopamine and norepinephrine and is often used when individuals experience sexual side effects from SSRIs, as it typically does not cause these issues. It's also used to aid in smoking cessation, which can be an added benefit. Mirtazapine works differently, increasing the release of norepinephrine and serotonin. It can be particularly helpful for individuals with depression who have trouble sleeping or need to gain weight, as it often promotes sleep and increases appetite.

The side effects of atypical antidepressants vary. Bupropion can cause insomnia and anxiety, whereas mirtazapine can cause sedation and weight gain. Personally, I found bupropion to be a good fit, especially since it did not affect my libido and helped me manage anxiety without making me feel overly sedated.

Navigating Side Effects and Finding the Right Fit

Finding the right antidepressant can be a trial-and-error process. It's essential to have open and ongoing communication with your healthcare provider, discussing any side effects and how the medication is affecting your daily life. Sometimes, the first medication you try may not be the right fit, and adjustments or changes may be necessary. It's also imperative to understand that antidepressants typically take several weeks to show their full effects. During this period, staying patient and maintaining regular check-ins with your doctor can help manage expectations and address any concerns that arise.

Incorporating medication into a broader treatment plan that includes therapy, lifestyle changes, and social support can significantly enhance the effectiveness of antidepressants. This holistic approach acknowledges that while medication can provide critical relief, managing depression often requires addressing multiple facets of one's life. As we continue exploring professional treatments and therapies, it's important to remember that medication is just one tool in the toolkit for managing depression. I must emphasize again that each individual's journey is unique, and finding the right combination of treatments can take time, but understanding the benefits and challenges of antidepressants can help make informed decisions and take proactive steps towards mental wellness.

Emerging Treatments

As traditional treatments for depression continue to be refined, new and innovative therapies are making their way into the mainstream. Emerging treatments like ketamine infusions and psychedelic-assisted therapy are offering hope to those who have not found relief through conventional methods. These cutting-edge approaches are changing the landscape of mental health care, providing new avenues for healing and recovery.

Ketamine Treatment

Ketamine, a medication traditionally used as an anesthetic, has recently gained attention for its rapid antidepressant effects. Unlike conventional antidepressants that can take weeks to show benefits, ketamine often works within hours. This makes it a game-changer for those with treatment-resistant depression or those experiencing acute suicidal ideation. Ketamine works by modulating the brain's glutamate system, which is involved in synaptic plasticity and neural communication. When administered in a controlled, clinical setting, typically via intravenous (IV) infusion, ketamine can lead to significant reductions in depressive symptoms. Patients often report feeling a sense of relief and clarity that has eluded them for years. A fellow patient described his experience with ketamine to me as "like a light switch being turned on in a dark room."

However, ketamine treatment is not without its pitfalls. The effects, while rapid, are often temporary, necessitating repeated infusions. Additionally, ketamine can cause dissociative side effects, where patients feel detached from their body or surroundings. In a clinical setting, these side effects are managed by experienced professionals, but they can be disorienting. Despite these challenges, ketamine's potential to provide quick relief has made it a valuable option, particularly for those in crisis. Research is ongoing to better understand the long-term effects and optimal protocols for its use. The hope is to harness ketamine's benefits while minimizing its risks, making it a viable part of the depression treatment arsenal.

Psychedelic-Assisted Therapy

Psychedelic-assisted therapy involves the use of substances like psilocybin (found in magic mushrooms) and MDMA (commonly known as ecstasy) in a therapeutic setting. These substances, once stigmatized and criminalized, are now being revisited for their potential to treat various mental health conditions, including depression.

Psychedelics work by profoundly altering consciousness and perception, which can lead to significant psychological insights and emotional breakthroughs. Psilocybin, for example, has been shown to reduce depressive symptoms by facilitating deep, often spiritual experiences that can shift a person's perspective on life and self. Patients often describe these experiences as deeply meaningful and transformative. On the other hand, MDMA-assisted therapy is showing promise in treating post-traumatic stress disorder (PTSD), which often coexists with depression. MDMA can enhance the therapeutic process by increasing feelings of safety and connection, allowing patients to process traumatic memories without being overwhelmed by fear or anxiety.

One of the most compelling aspects of psychedelic-assisted therapy is its potential to provide lasting benefits after just a few sessions. This is in stark contrast to traditional antidepressants, which must be taken daily and often for extended periods. However, the use of psychedelics in therapy is still in the experimental stage and is subject to rigorous clinical trials to ensure safety and efficacy.

The stories emerging from these trials are often remarkable. I remember reading about a veteran who had suffered from severe PTSD and depression for years. After a series of MDMA-assisted therapy sessions, he described feeling a sense of peace and closure he had never thought possible. Such accounts highlight the transformative potential of these therapies.

The Future of Depression Treatment

The integration of ketamine and psychedelic-assisted therapy into mainstream treatment protocols represents a paradigm shift in how we approach depression. These therapies are not just about symptom management; they aim to address the root causes of mental distress and facilitate deep, lasting healing. However, with innovation comes caution. Both ketamine and psychedelics require careful medical supervision and a structured therapeutic framework to be effective and safe. They are not magic bullets but tools that, when used appropriately, can significantly enhance the therapeutic process.

As we look to the future, ongoing research will be critical in refining these treatments and understanding their full potential. The possibilities are exciting, with numerous studies underway exploring new compounds, delivery methods, and therapeutic models. The emergence of these new treatments offers hope to those who have struggled with depression for years without finding relief. It shows the importance of continuing to push the boundaries of what is possible in mental health care. By embracing both the traditional and the innovative, we can build a more comprehensive and effective approach to treating depression.

As we move forward in this chapter, we'll explore how combining these emerging treatments with established therapies can provide a holistic and personalized approach to managing depression. By leveraging the best of both worlds, we can offer more tailored and effective care for those in need

COMBINING TREATMENTS

Depression is a condition with its claws buried in multiple facets that demand a nuanced treatment approach. A multidisciplinary strategy, which combines various treatments, can be highly effective in managing depression as it acknowledges that depression is not just a singular, isolated issue but a webbed interplay of biological, psychological, and social factors. Therefore, the best way to address depression is by integrating different therapies and treatments.

Combining treatments involves creating a personalized plan that might include medication, psychotherapy, lifestyle changes, and emerging therapies. This integrated approach ensures that each facet of the individual's depression is addressed, leading to more holistic healing.

A conventionally strong treatment scenario is where a person with depression is prescribed antidepressants to help manage their neurotransmitter imbalances. Alongside medication, they attend weekly CBT sessions to tackle negative thought patterns and behaviors. Additionally, they incorporate mindfulness practices and regular exercise into their routine. Each of these treatments on its own can be beneficial, but together, they create a synergistic effect, enhancing overall well-being.

Medication and Psychotherapy

Medication and psychotherapy are often considered the cornerstones of depression treatment. Antidepressants can help alleviate the biochemical aspects of depression, such as neurotransmitter imbalances, while psychotherapy addresses the psychological and behavioral components.

Personally, the combination of SSRIs and CBT proved invaluable to me. The medication provided the biochemical support I needed, lifting the weight just enough to allow me to engage effectively in therapy. Meanwhile, CBT helped me develop coping strategies and challenge negative thought patterns, creating a positive feedback loop that reinforced the benefits of both treatments.

Research supports this integrated approach as studies have shown that combining antidepressants with CBT can be more effective than either treatment alone, especially for severe depression. This combination not only improves depressive symptoms more quickly but also helps prevent relapse by equipping individuals with long-term coping mechanisms.

Adding Emerging Treatments

Incorporating emerging treatments like ketamine infusions or psychedelic-assisted therapy into a treatment plan can offer additional benefits, particularly for those with treatment-resistant depression. These therapies can provide rapid relief from symptoms, creating a window of opportunity for other treatments to take effect. For instance, consider a patient who has been struggling with severe depression for years, despite trying multiple medications and therapies. They begin a course of ketamine infusions, which quickly alleviate their most debilitating symptoms. With this newfound relief, they are better able to engage in psychotherapy and make lifestyle changes that were previously impossible due to the severity of their condition.

Emerging treatments can serve as a catalyst, jumpstarting the healing process and making it easier for individuals to benefit from other forms of therapy. However, it's important that these treatments are administered in a controlled, clinical setting, with ongoing support from mental health professionals to ensure safety and efficacy.

The Role of Lifestyle Changes

Lifestyle changes are pivotal in managing depression and can enhance the effectiveness of other treatments. Regular physical activity, a balanced diet, sufficient sleep, and stress management techniques are all critical components of a comprehensive treatment plan. Physical activity, for instance, has been shown to boost mood and reduce symptoms of depression by increasing endorphins and improving overall health. Diet also shows prominent results, with certain nutrients like omega-3 fatty acids and folate being linked to improved mood and cognitive function.

In my experience, integrating exercise and mindful eating into my routine made a substantial difference. The physical benefits of exercise were complemented by the mental clarity it provided, making it easier to engage in therapy and stick to my medication regimen. Similarly, a balanced diet helped stabilize my mood and energy levels, creating a more supportive foundation for healing. In essence, the intersection of different treatment options results in each option complementing the other.

Collaborative Care

A multidisciplinary approach requires collaboration among various healthcare providers. Psychiatrists, psychologists, therapists, primary care physicians, and even nutritionists and fitness trainers can all contribute in a comprehensive treatment plan. Regular communication and coordination among these professionals ensure that each aspect of the individual's care is aligned and complementary. This team-based approach not only enhances treatment effectiveness but also provides a robust support system for the individual. Imagine a scenario where a psychiatrist prescribes medication, a psychologist provides therapy, and a fitness trainer designs an exercise plan. They all collaborate to ensure that each component of the treatment is working harmoniously. This coordinated effort maximizes the benefits of each treatment and addresses the multifaceted nature of depression.

I understand that it might not be an option for many to collaborate with so many professionals despite having insurance, but the above depicts an idealized treatment scenario which can be mixed and matched to find the best possible configuration for you. In fact, one of the greatest strengths of a multidisciplinary approach is its flexibility. Treatment plans can be tailored to meet the unique needs of each individual, taking into account their specific symptoms, preferences, and lifestyle.

For some, a focus on medication and therapy might be most effective, while others might benefit more from incorporating mindfulness practices and physical activity. Emerging treatments can be added for those with treatment-resistant depression, providing a much-needed lifeline when traditional methods fall short. In my personal experience, finding the right combination of treatments was a process of trial and error. What worked for me might not work for someone else, and vice versa. The key is to remain open and flexible, willing to adjust the treatment plan as needed to find the most effective combination.

Combining treatments in a multidisciplinary approach offers a comprehensive and personalized path to managing depression by addressing the biological, psychological, and social aspects of the condition. This approach provides a more holistic and effective way to achieve long-term recovery. Exploring the benefits of integrating various treatments makes it clear that there is no one-size-fits-all solution to depression. Each person's journey is unique, and their treatment plan should reflect that. We can offer more tailored and effective care, helping individuals traverse the hardships of depression and find their way to healing by embracing a multidisciplinary approach.

In the next chapter, we will talk about lifestyle changes and coping strategies, exploring how adjustments in daily habits and routines can further support the journey toward mental well-being.

Depression can feel like a relentless storm, constantly battering the shores of our daily lives. But what if we could build a sturdy lighthouse, guiding us through the dark and turbulent waters? Lifestyle adjustments serve as that beacon, illuminating paths we might not have considered, and providing practical ways to manage the complications of depression. These adjustments aren't about quick fixes or magic bullets; they are about creating sustainable changes that build resilience and support long-term mental health.

When I first began my journey toward managing depression, the idea of altering my lifestyle seemed daunting. I was overwhelmed, unsure where to start, and skeptical about the impact such changes could have. However, as I gradually incorporated small, meaningful adjustments into my daily routine, I began to notice a shift. It wasn't an overnight transformation, but a slow, steady improvement that made life a bit more manageable. Trust me, these aren't all some theoretical mantras but rather pragmatic practices that I have personally integrated in my life to pull myself out of the miseries of depression; the same as I want for you.

One of the most significant realizations in this endeavor was the importance of social connections and support. Depression can be incredibly isolating, making it difficult to reach out and maintain relationships. However, building a supportive network can provide an essential buffer against the lows of depression. Whether it's through friends, family, or support groups, these connections offer empathy, understanding, and a sense of belonging. They remind us that we are not alone in our struggles and that there is always someone to lean on when the weight becomes too heavy.

Another critical area is making adjustments in our professional and academic lives. Managing depression in these settings can be challenging, but with the right strategies, it is possible to find a balance. This might involve setting realistic goals, seeking accommodations, or finding ways to reduce stress and avoid burnout by creating a work or school environment that acknowledges and accommodates our mental health needs for maneuvering these spaces more effectively.

Healthy coping mechanisms are central to how we manage daily stressors and emotional upheavals. It's essential to differentiate between healthy and unhealthy coping strategies. While some habits might offer temporary relief, they can ultimately exacerbate the problem. On the other hand, developing healthy coping mechanisms, such as mindfulness, exercise, and creative expression, can provide lasting benefits and improve overall well-being.

Long-term management of depression involves building resilience and preventing relapse. This is a dynamic, ongoing process that requires vigilance and adaptability by understanding our triggers, maintaining our support systems, and continuously refining our coping strategies. Developing resilience isn't about becoming invincible; it's about learning to bend without breaking, to face challenges with a mindset geared toward growth and recovery.

Going into this chapter, we will explore the various lifestyle adjustments that can make a significant difference in managing depression, examining the power of social connections and support, the importance of adjustments in professional and academic settings, the impact of coping mechanisms, and the strategies for long-term management. This chapter aims to provide you with the inspiration and mechanisms to make meaningful changes in your life.

I will remind you again, managing depression is a journey, not a destination. It's about finding what works for you, making incremental adjustments, and building a life that supports your mental health. These lifestyle changes might seem small, but collectively, they can create a powerful force for positive change, guiding you toward a more balanced and fulfilling life.

Depression often casts a shadow over our lives, making it challenging to connect with others and seek the support we need. However, building a supportive network can be a lifeline, providing us with the strength and resilience to walk the darkest paths. We, human beings, are inherently social creatures. We thrive on connection, and our relationships significantly influence our mental health. When we are depressed, isolation can seem like a refuge, but it often exacerbates our condition. Connecting with others can break this cycle of loneliness and despair. For instance, during your most challenging periods, reaching out to a close friend for a simple chat may lighten the burden you feel. The act of sharing, even if it is just a few words, makes a significant difference.

Family can be a heartfelt source of support. They are the people who have known us the longest, who often observe our struggles and history better than anyone else. However, family dynamics can be complex. It's essential to communicate openly with family members about your needs and boundaries. When I opened up to my family about my depression, it wasn't easy. But their willingness to listen and support me made a substantial impact. They didn't always know what to say or do, but their presence and willingness to aid me was extremely helpful.

Friends can provide a different kind of support. They are often our chosen family, people we trust and confide in. Peer support groups, both in-person and online, can also be incredibly beneficial. These groups consist of individuals who have faced similar challenges and can offer empathy and understanding. Joining a local support group for people with depression can be a transformative experience. Hearing others' stories and sharing your own helps you realize that you are not alone. The mutual support is comforting and empowering.

While personal relationships are vital, professional support is equally important. Therapists, counselors, and support workers can provide expert guidance and strategies to manage depression. They can help us understand our condition, develop coping mechanisms, and create a structured plan for recovery. Although I felt like I knew all the theoretical ins and outs of depression, my therapist became a cornerstone of my support network. Their professional insight and emotional support were invaluable in my healing process, making me realize that perhaps I didn't know as much as I thought I did and I wasn't even completely aware of my own potential strength and resilience.

Building a supportive network involves reaching out and allowing others to support you. It's about finding the right people and resources that resonate with you. Start with small steps. Reach out to a trusted friend or family member and share your feelings. Join a support group or online community where you can connect with others who understand what you're going through. Consider seeking professional help to add another layer of support.

In today's digital age, technology has become a building block of erecting and maintaining support networks. Online forums, social media groups, and mental health apps can connect you with a broader community. During the COVID-19 pandemic, virtual support became a lifeline for many. I found solace in online motivational groups and mental health forums, especially using websites like 7cups.com or betterhelp.com. These digital connections provided a sense of community when in-person interactions were limited.

Stigma around mental health can make it difficult to open up. Fear of judgment or misunderstanding may lead to hesitation. However, it's important to remember that seeking support is a sign of strength, not weakness. To overcome these challenges, start by educating yourself and others about depression. Share credible resources and information to reduce stigma and foster understanding.

Practical Tips

1. **Identify Key People**: Think about who in your life you trust and feel comfortable with. Reach out to them and express your need for support.

2. **Join Support Groups**: Look for local or online support groups. These communities can provide a safe space to share and connect.

3. **Use Technology**: Leverage apps and online platforms to find support networks and mental health resources.

4. **Set Boundaries**: It's okay to set boundaries with your support network. Communicate what you need and what is helpful for you.

5. **Be Patient**: Building a support network takes time. Be patient with yourself and others as you navigate this process.

One of the most captivating moments in my journey was when a friend simply sat with me in silence during a particularly rough day. No words were exchanged, but their presence was a powerful reminder that I wasn't alone. This experience taught me the importance of presence over perfection in supporting someone with depression. Sometimes, just being there is enough.

A supportive network can make a world of difference in managing depression. It provides a foundation of empathy, understanding, and practical help. By reaching out and allowing others into our journey, we can find the strength to face each day. Remember, building a support network is a step-by-step process. Each connection, no matter how small, is a step towards healing and resilience.

Managing depression in professional and academic settings is like rowing through a storm while trying to stay afloat. It's challenging, but with the right strategies and support, it's possible to maintain productivity and well-being. Depression can have a significant impact on both work and school performance. Concentration wanes, motivation dwindles, and the ability to handle stress diminishes. Imagine trying to climb a mountain with a heavy backpack, each step feeling more exhausting than the last. The first step towards making necessary adjustments for dealing with this is to recognize how depression affects your professional or academic life.

As I have repeatedly emphasized, open communication is critical. While you may feel hesitant to disclose your mental health struggles, doing so can lead to understanding and accommodations. I wish I had decided to talk to my employer about my depression, but unfortunately I was terrified of the judgment and misunderstanding. However, luckily for me, my manager was extremely supportive of my condition, recognizing the signs of my illness, and supporting me through my ailments on a day to day basis by the implementation of flexible work hours, shared workload, mental health days, etc.

I hope that you succeed where I failed and courageously have this conversation with your employer. When approaching this conversation, be clear about your needs. Explain how depression affects your work and suggest specific accommodations that could help. This might include flexible hours, a quieter workspace, or extended deadlines. Most employers and educators are willing to make reasonable accommodations if they understand the situation. Our inability to act due to anxiety or social stigma often don't let us take the necessary steps that we **_know_** are in the right direction.

Practical Adjustments

Flexible work hours can be a lifesaver. They allow you to manage your energy levels and work during times when you feel most productive. For instance, if mornings are particularly difficult, starting work later in the day can make a huge difference. A colleague of mine who suffered from depression, and consequently was often unable to get out of bed on account of drowsiness from his medication, was issued a note by his psychologist, urging the employer to allow working hour flexibility for him. Shifting his work hours to later in the day helped him balance his workload without compromising his mental health and continue to be a contributing member of the organization with revitalized vigor and dedication. I think this would be possible for a lot of us if only we mustered up the courage to speak up about our mental struggles in a constructive way.

Moreover, the option to work or study from home can provide a more comfortable and less stressful environment. The pandemic showed us that remote work and online classes are viable options. They eliminate the stress of commuting and allow for a more flexible schedule. However, it's essential to create a dedicated workspace to maintain boundaries between personal and professional or academic life. You don't want the pressures of your professional life to seep into your personal life, and vice versa.

Additionally, depression can make it challenging to handle a full workload. Prioritizing tasks and breaking them down into smaller, manageable steps can help. Consider a "one step at a time" approach. Start by focusing on the most critical tasks and gradually work your way through the list. This strategy prevents feeling overwhelmed and helps maintain productivity. As such, setting realistic and achievable goals is essential to take every step. Depression can distort our perception of what we can accomplish, leading to feelings of failure. Break down large tasks into smaller steps and celebrate small victories. Start setting smaller, more manageable goals, increasing your sense of accomplishment and boosting your confidence and motivation.

A supportive environment should be a priority for you; a metaphorical sanctuary. Surround yourself with understanding colleagues, friends, and classmates who can provide encouragement and assistance. This might involve joining a study group or a professional network. During your academic years, joining a study group provides not only academic support but also emotional support, knowing others are there for you. Taking regular breaks is essential to avoid burnout. Use these breaks to practice self-care activities that help you recharge. This might include a short walk, meditation, or listening to music. Incorporating these small breaks into my day helped manage stress levels and maintain focus. Here are some practical tips for managing depression at work and school:

1. **Plan and Prioritize**: Start each day by planning and prioritizing your tasks. Focus on the most important ones first.

2. **Use Tools and Apps**: Utilize productivity tools and apps to manage tasks and deadlines. Apps like Trello or Asana can help keep track of your workload.

3. **Stay Organized**: Keep your workspace organized to reduce stress and increase efficiency.

4. **Practice Mindfulness**: Incorporate mindfulness practices into your daily routine to help manage stress and stay focused.

5. **Take Breaks**: Schedule regular breaks throughout your day to rest and recharge.

6. **Set Boundaries**: Maintain boundaries between work, school, and personal life to avoid burnout.

Looking back, managing depression in professional and academic settings was one of the hardest challenges I faced. The fear of being judged, the constant battle with motivation, and the overwhelming pressure to perform were horrifying. However, through open communication, setting realistic goals, and utilizing support systems, I found a way to balance my responsibilities while taking care of my mental health. Each small adjustment made a significant difference, and over time, I learned to row through the storm more effectively.

As with all the other aspects off this invisible foe, managing depression in professional and academic settings requires a combination of strategies and support. The above tactics can make a substantial difference by maintaining productivity and mental well-being through the recognition of the impact of depression and making necessary adjustments. Remember, seeking help and making adjustments is not a sign of weakness, but a step towards resilience and recovery.

Coping Mechanisms

As I stipulated before, having depression is like rowing through a turbulent sea. Some days, the waves are manageable, and you can keep your head above water. Other days, it feels like you're drowning. How you cope with these turbulent times can make a significant difference in your journey towards recovery. As such, healthy coping strategies are like lifebuoys, keeping you afloat and helping you navigate the storm. These strategies not only provide immediate relief but also contribute to long-term resilience. Most of the healthy coping mechanism that we can incorporate in our lives have already been discussed throughout this book, but I will reiterate them so you can visualize everything in context:

1. **Exercise:** Engaging in regular physical activity is a powerful tool against depression. Exercise releases endorphins, the body's natural mood lifters, which can help alleviate symptoms of depression. Even a simple walk in the park can make a difference. I understand that there are days when getting out of bed feels impossible, but pushing yourself to go for a walk brings a subtle yet noticeable improvement in your mood.

2. **Mindfulness and Meditation:** Mindfulness practices, such as meditation and deep breathing exercises which we discussed in chapter 5, can help manage the symptoms of depression. They encourage a focus on the present moment, reducing the ruminative thoughts that often accompany depression. Techniques like guided meditation or yoga can provide a calming effect, helping to reduce stress and anxiety. Incorporating mindfulness into your daily routine helps create a sense of calm amidst the chaos.

3. **Creative Outlets:** Engaging in creative activities like painting, writing, or playing music can serve as an emotional release. These activities allow for self-expression and can be therapeutic. Journaling, in particular, has been a valuable tool for me. Pouring my thoughts onto paper helped me process my emotions and gain clarity. For you, it can help you do the same, or perhaps, even more.

4. **Social Support:** As I keep repeating, building and maintaining a strong support network is very important. Connecting with friends, family, or support groups provides a sense of belonging and understanding. Reaching out to friends and family makes a world of difference even when you don't want to. Knowing that

you aren't alone in your struggles provides comfort and strength in your most desperate moments.

5. **Professional Help:** Seeking help from a mental health professional, such as a therapist or counselor, can provide structured support. Therapists can offer techniques and strategies tailored to your specific needs, helping you develop healthy coping mechanisms. Therapists provide invaluable guidance, helping one traverse the darkest times with practical strategies and structured support.

6. **Healthy Lifestyle Choices:** Maintaining a healthy lifestyle, including a balanced diet and adequate sleep, can significantly impact mental health. A nutritious diet fuels your body and mind, while sufficient sleep helps regulate mood and cognitive functions. Personally, prioritizing sleep and self-care played a game-changing role in managing my symptoms.

Unhealthy Coping Strategies

Unhealthy coping mechanisms can provide temporary relief but often exacerbate the problem in the long run. These strategies can lead to a cycle of self-destruction, making it harder to break free from the grips of depression.

1. **Substance Abuse:** Turning to alcohol or drugs to numb the pain is a common but dangerous coping mechanism. While these substances might provide temporary relief, they can worsen depression and lead to addiction. I witnessed friends fall into this trap, only to find themselves deeper in despair and struggling with additional issues like dependency and health problems.

2. **Self-Harm:** As discussed in Chapter 4, some individuals resort to self-harm as a way to cope with overwhelming emotions. This behavior can provide a temporary sense of control or release but ultimately

leads to more harm and perpetuates the cycle of depression. It's extremely important to seek help if you're engaging in self-harm; there are healthier ways to manage emotions.

3. **Isolation:** Withdrawing from social interactions might seem like a way to avoid the stress of engaging with others, but isolation often deepens feelings of loneliness and despair. Cutting off social connections can deprive you of the support and understanding needed to navigate depression. I learned the hard way that retreating into isolation only made my struggles more intense.

4. **Overworking:** Some individuals immerse themselves in work or studies to avoid dealing with their emotions. While staying busy can distract you from your feelings temporarily, it can lead to burnout and increased stress. Balancing work with self-care is essential to prevent exacerbating depression.

5. **Negative Self-Talk:** Engaging in negative self-talk, where you constantly criticize and belittle yourself, can reinforce feelings of worthlessness and hopelessness. This destructive inner dialogue can create a self-fulfilling prophecy, making it harder to see any positive aspects of life. Challenging and reframing these thoughts is absolutely essential for developing a healthier mindset.

Understanding the difference between healthy and unhealthy coping mechanisms is necessary for managing depression effectively. It's about recognizing what helps in the long run versus what might provide immediate relief but ultimately harms you. Balancing these strategies requires self-awareness and sometimes, the guidance of a professional. I personally employed a mix of both healthy and unhealthy coping strategies. There were times when I leaned on unhealthy mechanisms out of sheer desperation, including self-harm. However, the turning point came when I started incorporating healthier strategies into my routine. The shift wasn't immediate, but gradually, the healthier habits started to take root, providing a stronger foundation for my mental health. Frankly speaking, even if it seems like a distant dream now, it's only after we fully embrace the healthy coping mechanisms that we start seeing positive long-term results.

Successfully regaining control back from depression demands adherence to healthy coping mechanisms. You can build resilience and improve your mental well-being by identifying and adopting healthy strategies while steering clear of destructive ones. Always remember, it's a journey, and finding what works best for you is a continuous process. Surround yourself with supportive individuals, seek professional help when needed, and be patient with yourself. With the right coping mechanisms, managing depression becomes a more attainable goal.

Chapter 8: Strategies for Holistic Depression Management

In our journey through understanding and managing depression, we've explored the biology, psychology, and impact of depression on daily life. We've delved into self-help techniques, professional treatments, and lifestyle changes that can aid in managing this condition. Now, let's bring these elements together into a comprehensive, pragmatic strategy for dealing with depression. This chapter aims to provide a structured, holistic approach that synthesizes the insights from previous chapters, offering a basic structure of a one-size-fits-all strategy where we will leave room for personalized adjustments for a tailored approach.

Establishing a Daily Routine

Creating a consistent daily routine is foundational in managing depression. Regular schedules provide structure, reduce uncertainty, and can improve sleep patterns.

Morning Rituals: Start the day with activities that promote a positive mindset. This could include light exercise, mindfulness meditation, or a healthy breakfast. For instance, beginning your day with a few minutes of deep breathing exercises can set a calm tone for the hours ahead. Incorporating stretches or a short walk can invigorate your body and mind. Research suggests that exposure to natural light in the morning can regulate circadian rhythms, enhancing mood and energy levels throughout the day. Consider spending a few minutes outside or near a window to soak in natural sunlight.

Work and Leisure Balance: Incorporate periods of focused work or tasks followed by leisure activities. This balance helps maintain productivity without overwhelming stress. Allocate specific times for work, breaks, and personal time, ensuring you have moments to unwind and recharge. Time-blocking can be an effective method to ensure that you maintain a balanced schedule. Use a planner or digital calendar to map out your day, clearly marking periods for work, rest, and recreational activities. This can help in managing tasks efficiently and reducing the sense of being overwhelmed.

Evening Wind-Down: Establish calming evening routines to prepare the mind and body for restful sleep. This might involve reading, gentle yoga, or listening to soothing music. Dim the lights, avoid screens an hour before bed, and create a serene environment to signal your body it's time to relax. Implementing a technology curfew, turning off electronic devices an hour before bed, can significantly improve sleep quality. Engage in relaxing activities like journaling or taking a warm bath to signal your body that it's time to wind down

Self-Help Techniques and Mindfulness

Building on the self-help strategies discussed earlier, integrating mindfulness and cognitive behavioral techniques can significantly enhance emotional regulation and resilience.

Mindfulness Meditation: Regular practice helps in staying grounded and reduces symptoms of anxiety and stress. Apps and guided sessions can be valuable resources. Engage in daily mindfulness exercises, focusing on your breath or a simple mantra to center your thoughts and emotions. Studies have shown that mindfulness can alter brain structure, enhancing areas associated with self-regulation and reducing those linked with stress. Start with short, manageable sessions, gradually increasing the duration as you become more comfortable with the practice.

Journaling: Keeping a daily journal to track emotions, thoughts, and triggers provides insights and aids in managing negative thinking patterns. Documenting your feelings and experiences can offer clarity and help you identify recurring themes or stressors. A practice known as "expressive writing" can be particularly beneficial, where you write freely about your deepest thoughts and emotions. This can help in processing complex feelings and gaining a new perspective on challenges.

Positive Affirmations: Incorporating positive affirmations into daily life can reinforce self-worth and combat negative self-talk. Begin each day by repeating affirmations that resonate with you, such as "I am capable," "I am resilient," and "I am worthy." Research indicates that positive affirmations can activate brain areas associated with self-related processing and reward, helping to foster a positive self-image and counteract depressive thoughts.

Leveraging Professional Treatments

Knowing the spectrum of professional treatments available is essential for comprehensive care.

Therapy: CBT, Dialectical Behavior Therapy (DBT), and other modalities can be tailored to individual needs. Regular sessions with a qualified therapist help in addressing underlying issues and developing coping strategies. Therapy provides a safe space to explore your thoughts and feelings with professional guidance. Other therapeutic approaches like Interpersonal Therapy (IPT) and Acceptance and Commitment Therapy (ACT) can also be beneficial. IPT focuses on improving interpersonal relationships and social functioning, while ACT encourages accepting negative emotions as part of the human experience and committing to positive behaviors despite these feelings.

Medication: For some, antidepressant medications may be necessary. It's important to follow a healthcare provider's guidance and report any side effects or concerns. Medications like SSRIs, SNRIs, or tricyclic antidepressants can help balance brain chemistry and alleviate symptoms. Regular follow-ups with your healthcare provider are essential to monitor the effectiveness of the medication and make adjustments as needed. It's also important to be aware of potential side effects and communicate any concerns to your doctor promptly.

Support Groups: Engaging with support groups provides community and shared experiences, reducing the sense of isolation that often accompanies depression. Sharing your journey with others who understand can offer comfort and new perspectives. Support groups can be found locally through community centers or online platforms. These groups provide a space to share experiences, offer and receive support, and learn from others who are facing similar challenges. They can also provide valuable information about resources and strategies for managing depression

Lifestyle Changes and Coping Strategies

Sustainable lifestyle changes are integral to long-term management of depression.

Nutrition: A balanced diet rich in omega-3 fatty acids, vitamins, and minerals supports brain health. Consider consulting a nutritionist for personalized advice. Foods like salmon, walnuts, leafy greens, and whole grains can boost mental and physical well-being. Omega-3 fatty acids, found in fatty fish, flaxseeds, and walnuts, are particularly beneficial for brain health. These nutrients help in reducing inflammation and promoting the production of neurotransmitters that regulate mood. Additionally, a diet high in fruits, vegetables, and whole grains can improve overall health and energy levels, further supporting mental well-being.

Exercise: Regular physical activity, even in moderate amounts, can boost mood and energy levels. Activities like walking, swimming, or yoga are excellent choices. Exercise releases endorphins, the body's natural mood lifters, and can improve overall health. Aim for at least 30 minutes of moderate exercise most days of the week. Engaging in group activities or classes can also provide social interaction and additional motivation. Studies have shown that exercise can be as effective as medication for some people in managing symptoms of depression, highlighting its importance as a cornerstone of depression management.

Sleep Hygiene: Prioritizing good sleep hygiene by maintaining a regular sleep schedule, creating a restful environment, and avoiding stimulants before bedtime is essential. Establish a consistent bedtime routine, keep your bedroom cool and dark, and limit caffeine and alcohol intake. Sleep disturbances are common in depression, so ensuring good sleep hygiene is important. Techniques like maintaining a regular sleep-wake schedule, creating a comfortable sleep environment, and practicing relaxation techniques before bed can help improve sleep quality and duration.

Building a Support System

A robust support system is critical in tackling the challenges of depression. This involves both personal relationships and community resources.

Communication: Open and honest communication with friends and family about one's struggles and needs creates understanding and support. Sharing your experiences can help loved ones understand your condition and how they can assist you. Regularly updating your support network on your progress and any changes in your needs can help maintain effective and supportive relationships.

Community Involvement: Engaging in community activities or volunteer work can provide a sense of purpose and connection. Joining clubs, participating in local events, or volunteering can expand your social network and offer fulfilling experiences. Community involvement can also provide opportunities for personal growth and development, enhancing self-esteem and reducing feelings of isolation.

Professional Support: Regular check-ins with healthcare providers ensure that the treatment plan remains effective and adjustments can be made as necessary. Consistent medical and therapeutic support can monitor progress and address any emerging issues. Having a healthcare team that includes your primary care physician, therapist, and possibly a psychiatrist can provide comprehensive and coordinated care. Regular appointments and open communication with your healthcare team can help ensure that all aspects of your treatment are aligned and effective

Monitoring Progress and Adjusting Strategies

Regularly assessing the effectiveness of the adopted strategies is important for ongoing improvement and adaptation.

Self-Assessment: Periodic self-assessments help in recognizing progress and identifying areas needing adjustment. Reflect on your journey, noting improvements and areas still causing difficulties. Keeping a journal or using a tracking app can help you monitor your symptoms, identify triggers, and evaluate the effectiveness of different strategies over time.

Professional Feedback: Regular consultations with therapists and doctors to review progress and make necessary changes to the treatment plan. Professional input can provide new strategies and reinforce successful approaches. It's important to communicate openly with your healthcare providers about what is and isn't working. They can provide valuable insights and adjustments to your treatment plan based on their expertise and your feedback.

Adaptability: Being open to trying new approaches and adjusting existing ones based on what works best for individual circumstances. Flexibility in your treatment plan allows for more effective management of depression. Life circumstances and symptoms can change over time, so being adaptable and willing to try new strategies is essential. This might include exploring new therapies, adjusting medication, or incorporating new self-help techniques into your routine.

A Personalized Plan through Integrative Approach

Every individual's experience with depression is unique, and therefore, the management plan must be tailored to personal needs and preferences. Here's a detailed approach to creating a personalized plan:

1. Initial Assessment: Start with a comprehensive assessment of your current state. This includes understanding your symptoms, triggers, and the impact of depression on various aspects of your life. Tools like the Beck Depression Inventory (BDI) or Patient Health Questionnaire (PHQ-9) can provide a baseline measure of your symptoms.

2. Setting Goals: Identify short-term and long-term goals for your mental health. These goals should be Specific, Measurable, Achievable, Relevant, and Time-bound (SMART). For example, a short-term goal might be to improve sleep quality, while a long-term goal could be to reduce overall symptoms of depression by 50% within six months.

3. Developing a Routine: Based on your assessment, develop a daily routine that includes elements discussed earlier. Ensure that your routine is realistic and allows for flexibility. For instance, if mornings are particularly difficult, schedule more relaxing activities during that time and gradually increase activity levels as the day progresses.

4. Self-Help Strategies: Incorporate self-help techniques that resonate with you. This could include mindfulness exercises, journaling, or positive affirmations. Experiment with different methods to find what works best for you. Regularly review and adjust these practices to keep them effective and engaging.

5. Professional Treatment: Engage with healthcare providers to establish a professional treatment plan. This might include regular therapy sessions, medication, or other therapeutic interventions. Ensure that you have a clear understanding of your treatment plan, including the purpose and expected outcomes of each component.

6. Lifestyle Modifications: Implement lifestyle changes that support your mental health. This includes a balanced diet, regular exercise, and good sleep hygiene. Make gradual changes to avoid feeling overwhelmed. For instance, start with incorporating one healthy meal a day and slowly build up to a full balanced diet.

7. Building Support: Develop a robust support system by communicating with friends, family, and engaging in community activities. Identify key individuals in your support network and establish regular check-ins with them. Consider joining support groups to connect with others who understand your experience.

8. Monitoring and Adjustment: Regularly assess your progress using self-assessment tools and feedback from healthcare providers. Be prepared to adjust your plan as needed. Celebrate small victories and learn from setbacks. Keeping a detailed journal or using a mental health app can help track your progress and provide valuable insights for adjustments.

A holistic and adaptable plan for managing depression can be formulated by integrating strategies from self-help techniques, professional treatments, and lifestyle changes. This approach not only addresses the symptoms of depression but also empowers individuals to regain control over their lives and well-being.

By now you must have read this quite a few times, but I will repeat it yet again; managing depression is a journey that requires patience, resilience, and a willingness to seek and accept help. Together, we can walk this path and find the light at the end of the tunnel. Managing depression demands a multipronged approach. It's *essential* to understand that what works for one person might not work for another, so if my experiences do not resonate with you, do not lose hope. Be patient and persistent in finding the right combination of strategies that work for you.

FINDING PEACE AND PURPOSE

Depression can feel like a bottomless pit, a place so dark and deep that light seems like a distant memory. But it's within this darkness that the most profound transformations can occur. My journey through depression has been arduous, but it has also been a path to self-discovery and a deeper understanding of life's purpose and meaning. In this chapter, I want to share how finding purpose and meaning has been the guiding light out of my depression, leading to a lasting sense of fulfillment and peace.

As I reflect on my journey out of the depths of depression, I am struck by the transformative power of finding purpose and meaning in life. This chapter is a testament to that journey, detailing how understanding happiness in the little moments and finding peace in the spaces between joy and sorrow have brought me an unparalleled sense of fulfillment. My realization that happiness is a fleeting emotion but a consistent peace of mind is eternal has illuminated my path in ways I never imagined.

Depression, with its suffocating grip and unrelenting darkness, seemed unescapable at times. It robbed me of joy, sapped my energy, and clouded my thoughts. Yet, in the midst of this turmoil, a guiding light emerged, a sense of purpose that slowly began to illuminate the shadows. This light was not a sudden revelation but a gradual awakening, sparked by moments of clarity and the pursuit of something greater than my pain.

In the darkest moments, when despair seemed to consume every ounce of my being, I discovered that the search for meaning provided a glimmer of hope. It was a beacon that called to me, urging me to look beyond my suffering and to seek out the deeper currents of life. This journey was not about escaping my pain but about understanding it, integrating it, and using it as a catalyst for growth and transformation.

One of the most profound realizations I had on this journey was that happiness is not a constant state but a collection of fleeting moments. These moments, often small and seemingly insignificant, hold immense power. The warmth of the sun on my face, the sound of laughter shared with a friend, the beauty of a sunset, these are the instances that, when acknowledged and cherished, tie the knots of joy throughout our lives.

Depression often blinds us to these moments, overshadowing them with darkness. Yet, as I began to pay attention to these fleeting sparks of happiness, I found that they accumulated, creating a reservoir of joy that I could draw upon even in the bleakest times. This shift in perspective taught me to savor the present, to find beauty in the mundane, and to appreciate the transient nature of happiness.

Alongside these moments of happiness, I discovered the entrancing peace that exists in the spaces between joy and sorrow. Life is a continuous ebb and flow of emotions, and in this rhythm, there is a serene stillness that offers solace and stability. This peace is not tied to external circumstances but arises from within, from a deep acceptance of life's inherent uncertainties and imperfections.

Finding peace in these interstitial spaces required a shift in mindset. I learned to embrace the full spectrum of my emotions, recognizing that each feeling, whether joyful or painful, had a place in my life. I created room for peace to take root by allowing myself to experience emotions without judgment. This peace became a constant companion, a grounding force that steadied me through life's highs and lows.

Happiness, I came to understand, is a fleeting emotion, while peace of mind is a more enduring state. This realization was a turning point in my journey. It shifted my focus from the pursuit of constant happiness, which is inherently elusive, to the cultivation of a consistent peace of mind. This peace, born of acceptance and mindfulness, provided a sense of stability and fulfillment that transcended the transient nature of happiness.

Peace of mind is not the absence of struggle but the presence of a calm center that remains steadfast amidst life's chaos. It is the ability to remain grounded, to respond rather than react, and to find clarity even in confusion. This inner peace has become a sanctuary, a place of refuge where I can return whenever the storms of life threaten to overwhelm me.

A significant part of my journey towards finding purpose and meaning has been the liberation I found through writing. What began as a simple act of journaling transformed into a powerful tool for self-expression and healing. Writing allowed me to articulate my thoughts, process my emotions, and explore the depths of my mind. It became a mirror reflecting my innermost self, providing insights that were otherwise hidden.

Journaling was my initial foray into writing, a private space where I could pour out my soul without fear of judgment. It was through this practice that I discovered the cathartic power of putting pen to paper. As my thoughts flowed, I began to untangle the knots within my mind, gaining clarity and understanding. This process was liberating, freeing me from the confines of my thoughts and opening up new avenues of self-discovery.

Parallel to my journey in writing was my exploration of reading and understanding various philosophies of the world. Books became my companions, offering wisdom, solace, and a broader perspective on life. Through the words of philosophers, poets, and thinkers, I found guidance and inspiration. They challenged my beliefs, expanded my horizons, and helped me find my place in the world.

Philosophy, in particular, played a crucial role in shaping my understanding of meaning and purpose. Existentialism, with its emphasis on individual freedom and responsibility, resonated deeply with me. The idea that we are responsible for creating our own meaning in an indifferent universe was both daunting and empowering. It challenged me to take ownership of my life and to actively seek out what gave it purpose.

As I immersed myself in writing and philosophical exploration, I began to notice a heartfelt shift within me. The heavy shroud of depression slowly lifted, replaced by a sense of fulfillment and joy that was not dependent on external circumstances. This transformation was not an overnight miracle but a gradual process, marked by small victories and moments of clarity.

The concept of "destination addiction," the belief that happiness lies in the next job, the next relationship, the next achievement, had kept me in a perpetual state of dissatisfaction. But as I let go of this notion, I discovered the joy of living in the present. I learned to appreciate the journey rather than fixating on the destination. This shift in perspective brought a sense of peace and contentment that I had never experienced before.

Looking back, I realize that my struggle with depression was not a detour but an integral part of my journey. It was through this struggle that I discovered the depth of my resilience, the power of vulnerability, and the importance of finding meaning and purpose. Without depression, I might never have embarked on this path of self-discovery, nor would I have experienced the profound peace that now permeates my being.

This journey has taught me that life is not about the absence of pain but about finding meaning in the midst of it. It is about embracing our struggles, learning from them, and using them as a catalyst for growth. It is about finding joy in the little moments and peace in the spaces between. It is about living with purpose, guided by our passions and values.

Pursuing my passion for writing has been one of the most liberating and fulfilling experiences of my life. Writing has not only been a form of self-expression but also a means of connecting with others. It has allowed me to share my story, to offer support and encouragement to those who may be struggling, and to contribute to the broader conversation about mental health.

Passion is a powerful force that drives us to explore, create, and grow. It is the fire that fuels our pursuit of purpose and meaning. When we engage in activities that we are passionate about, we tap into a wellspring of energy and creativity. Passion gives our lives direction and significance, guiding us towards our true calling.

The philosophical teachings I have encountered on this journey have been invaluable in shaping my understanding of purpose and meaning. Existentialist philosophers like Jean-Paul Sartre and Viktor Frankl emphasized the importance of creating our own meaning in a world that is inherently meaningless. Their ideas resonated deeply with me, providing a framework for understanding my own experiences.

Viktor Frankl's concept of "logotherapy," which focuses on finding meaning in life even in the face of suffering, was particularly impactful. Frankl, a Holocaust survivor, argued that our primary drive in life is not pleasure, as Freud suggested, but the pursuit of what we find meaningful. This idea reinforced my belief that purpose is a central component of mental well-being and resilience.

Self-discovery is an ongoing journey, one that requires continuous reflection, exploration, and growth. It is a process of peeling back the layers of our psyche to uncover our true selves. This journey involves confronting our fears, embracing our vulnerabilities, and celebrating our strengths. It is about understanding who we are at our core and what drives us.

Throughout this journey, I have learned to listen to my inner voice, to trust my intuition, and to follow my passions. I have discovered that self-discovery is not a solitary endeavor but one that is enhanced by our interactions with others. It is through our relationships, our experiences, and our reflections that we gain insights into ourselves.

Vulnerability has been a recurring theme in my journey towards finding purpose and meaning. It is the courage to be open, to be honest, and to be authentic. Vulnerability allows us to connect with others on a deeper level, fostering empathy and understanding. It is through vulnerability that we build meaningful relationships and create a sense of community.

Embracing vulnerability means acknowledging our fears and insecurities, allowing ourselves to be seen, and taking the risk of being hurt. It is about letting go of the need for perfection and accepting ourselves as we are. Vulnerability is not a sign of weakness but a testament to our strength and resilience. It is a powerful tool for healing and growth.

Resilience is the ability to bounce back from adversity, to keep moving forward despite the obstacles, and to find strength in the face of challenges. It is a quality that we develop through our experiences, our struggles, and our triumphs. Resilience is not about avoiding pain but about facing it head-on and emerging stronger.

My journey through depression has taught me the value of resilience. It has shown me that even in the darkest moments, there is a light that guides us forward. Resilience is about finding the courage to rise each time we fall, to learn from our experiences, and to use them as stepping stones towards growth. It is about believing in ourselves and our ability to overcome whatever life throws our way.

One of the most important lessons I have learned on this journey is that meaning can be found even in the midst of pain. Our struggles, our losses, and our challenges are not meaningless but opportunities for growth and transformation. We can transcend it, turning pain into wisdom and despair into hope, by finding meaning in our suffering.

This process of finding meaning in pain requires a shift in perspective. It involves viewing our struggles not as obstacles but as opportunities for growth. It is about asking ourselves what we can learn from our experiences and how we can use them to become better, stronger, and more compassionate individuals. This shift in perspective allows us to transform our pain into a source of strength and resilience.

As we conclude this chapter, I want to remind you that the journey towards finding purpose and meaning is ongoing. It is a lifelong process of learning, growing, and evolving. There will be moments of triumph and moments of challenge, but each step forward is a testament to your strength and resilience.

The Way Forward

As I bring this book to a close, I am thinking about the turbulent, but enlightening journey we've just traversed together. Throughout these pages, we have walked the maze of depression, anxiety, and the deep-seated search for meaning in an often bewildering world. We have dived into the depths of despair and ascended toward the light of understanding, each step revealing more about the delicate balance of our minds and souls.

This book has been a reflection of my experiences, my thoughts, and my struggles. I have opened my heart to you, the reader, in the hope that my story may resonate with you, that it may offer a glimmer of hope or a sense of companionship. Writing this book has been a journey of healing for me, and I hope reading it has been a journey of healing for you.

Our exploration began with the acknowledgment of our struggles, recognizing that the path to healing starts with acceptance. We have dissected the various facets of mental health, understanding that depression is not merely a clinical condition but a profound existential experience that shapes our perception of reality. This journey has not been about finding a quick fix or a definitive cure but about embracing the continuous process of self-discovery and growth.

Self-discovery is not a destination but a journey, an ongoing process of peeling back the layers of our psyche to understand who we truly are. It involves looking deeply into the mirror of our soul, acknowledging our flaws and fears, and embracing our strengths and aspirations. This journey is often uncomfortable, sometimes painful, but always transformative.

It is through self-discovery that we find our true selves, our passions, and our purpose.

One of the central themes we have encountered is the power of vulnerability. In a society that often equates vulnerability with weakness, we have discovered its true strength. By opening up about our deepest fears and insecurities, we forge connections that transcend superficial interactions. These connections remind us that we are not alone in our struggles and that our shared experiences can be a source of immense comfort and strength.

Vulnerability is the cornerstone of authentic living. It is the courage to be seen, to be honest about our fears and insecurities. When we embrace vulnerability, we open ourselves to deeper connections and more meaningful relationships. We find that our struggles are not unique but shared by many, and this shared experience fosters a sense of community and belonging. Vulnerability is not a sign of weakness but a testament to our strength, our resilience, and our capacity for love and connection.

Resilience has been another key pillar of our journey. We have learned that resilience is not about never falling but about rising each time we do. It's about finding the courage to face our darkest moments, knowing that these moments do not define us. Through resilience, we transform pain into wisdom, fear into courage, and despair into hope. Each setback becomes a stepping stone, guiding us towards a deeper understanding of ourselves and the world around us.

Resilience is the ability to withstand adversity and bounce back stronger than before. It is the tenacity to keep moving forward despite the obstacles, the setbacks, and the pain. Resilience is not something we are born with; it is something we cultivate through our experiences, our struggles, and our triumphs. It is the inner strength that propels us forward, the unwavering belief that we can overcome whatever life throws our way.

Finding purpose and meaning in life has been a recurrent theme. We have explored how a sense of purpose can act as a beacon, guiding us through the fog of depression. Whether it is through creative expression, helping others, or pursuing a passion, purpose gives our lives direction and significance. It anchors us, providing a reason to persevere even when the journey seems insurmountable.

Purpose is the driving force behind our actions, the reason we get out of bed each morning. It is what gives our lives meaning and direction. Without purpose, we drift aimlessly, lost in the sea of life. But with purpose, we find our way, we navigate the storms, and we reach our destination. Purpose is not something we find; it is something we create. It is born out of our passions, our values, and our desire to make a difference in the world.

Beyond the individual, our journey also extends beyond the personal realm, touching upon the collective responsibility we share in addressing mental health. As a society, we must strive to create environments that nurture understanding, support, and compassion. By breaking the stigma surrounding mental health, we pave the way for more open and honest conversations. We create a world where seeking help is seen as a sign of strength, and where every individual feels valued and heard.

Mental health is not just an individual issue; it is a collective responsibility. We all have a role to play in creating a society that supports mental well-being. This involves educating ourselves and others about mental health, challenging the stigma and stereotypes, and advocating for better mental health services. It involves creating environments where people feel safe to speak up, to seek help, and to support one another. Together, we can create a world where mental health is prioritized, where everyone feels valued and supported.

As we look ahead, let us carry with us the lessons learned and the insights gained. The journey towards mental well-being is ongoing, with each day offering new opportunities for growth and understanding. Let us embrace this journey with hope and determination, knowing that every step forward, no matter how small, is a triumph.

Hope is the light that guides us through the darkness. It is the belief that things can and will get better. Even in our darkest moments, hope keeps us going, giving us the strength to keep moving forward. Hope is not a passive state but an active process. It involves setting goals, making plans, and taking action. It involves believing in ourselves and in our ability to overcome whatever challenges come our way. With hope, we can face the future with confidence and optimism.

In writing this book, I have not only shared my thoughts and experiences but have also walked my own journey of healing and self-discovery. I have confronted my own vulnerabilities and found solace in the realization that we are all connected through our shared humanity. My hope is that this book has provided you with a sense of companionship, a reminder that you are never alone in your struggles.

This book has been a labor of love, a reflection of my journey through the valleys and peaks of mental health. It has been a process of healing, of understanding, and of growth. I have poured my heart and soul into these pages, sharing my deepest fears, my greatest triumphs, and my ongoing struggles. Through this process, I have come to realize that our stories, though unique, are interconnected. We are all part of the same human tribe, related together by our shared experiences and emotions. My hope is that this book has resonated with you, offering you comfort, inspiration, and a sense of companionship.

To everyone who has journeyed with me through these pages, I extend my deepest gratitude. Your willingness to explore these difficult topics is a testament to your courage and resilience. As we move forward, let us continue to support one another, to listen with empathy, and to strive for a world where mental well-being is a universal priority.

As we conclude this book, I want to leave you with a message of hope and encouragement. Life is a journey, filled with ups and downs, triumphs and challenges. It is a journey of self-discovery, of growth, and of transformation. No matter where you are on your journey, know that you are not alone. There is always hope, always a reason to keep moving forward. Together, we can create a world where mental well-being is prioritized, where everyone feels valued and supported. Let us walk this path with hope in our hearts and a commitment to embrace the journey, no matter where it leads.

The Importance of Community

One of the most important aspects of our journey has been the discovery of community. We have learned that healing is not a solitary endeavor but a collective one. It is through our connections with others that we find strength, support, and understanding. Community provides us with a sense of belonging, reminding us that we are not alone in our struggles.

In our journey together, we have explored the importance of building and nurturing supportive communities. Whether it is through friends, family, support groups, or online communities, these connections are vital to our mental well-being. They provide us with a network of support, a safe space to share our thoughts and feelings, and a source of encouragement and inspiration. As we move forward, let us continue to build and strengthen these connections, fostering a sense of community and belonging.

The Power of Mindfulness

Mindfulness has also been a recurring theme in our journey. By focusing on the present moment and cultivating awareness, we can reduce stress, improve our mental well-being, and find greater peace and contentment. Mindfulness allows us to break free from the cycle of negative thoughts and emotions, giving us the space to breathe, reflect, and grow.

Mindfulness is not just a practice but a way of life. It involves being fully present in each moment, accepting our thoughts and feelings without judgment, and approaching life with a sense of curiosity and openness. Through mindfulness, we can develop a deeper understanding of ourselves and our experiences, finding clarity and peace amidst the chaos. As we continue our journey, let us embrace the power of mindfulness, cultivating awareness and presence in our daily lives.

Embracing Change

Change is an inevitable part of life, and our journey has been marked by moments of transformation and growth. We have learned that change, though often challenging, is also an opportunity for renewal and reinvention. By embracing change, we open ourselves to new possibilities, new experiences, and new ways of being.

Change can be daunting, especially when it involves stepping out of our comfort zones and facing the unknown. But it is through change that we grow, evolve, and discover our true potential. Embracing change requires courage, resilience, and a willingness to let go of the past. It involves trusting in the process and believing in our ability to navigate whatever comes our way. As we move forward, let us embrace change with an open heart and an adventurous spirit, knowing that each new chapter brings with it the potential for growth and transformation.

Finding Balance

In our journey towards mental well-being, finding balance has been a crucial aspect. We have explored the importance of balancing our physical, emotional, and mental needs, recognizing that each aspect of our being is interconnected. By finding balance, we create harmony within ourselves and our lives.

Balance is about finding the right equilibrium between work and rest, activity and relaxation, giving and receiving. It involves prioritizing our well-being, setting boundaries, and making time for the things that nourish our body, mind, and soul. Finding balance is an ongoing process, requiring us to continuously assess and adjust our lives to ensure we are meeting our needs. As we continue our journey, let us strive for balance, creating a life that is both fulfilling and sustainable.

The Journey Continues

As we conclude this book, I want to remind you that the journey towards mental well-being is ongoing. It is a lifelong process of learning, growing, and evolving. There will be moments of triumph and moments of challenge, but each step forward is a testament to your strength and resilience.

Remember that you are not alone on this journey. Reach out for support when you need it, offer support to others, and continue to cultivate a sense of community and connection. Embrace vulnerability, practice resilience, and find purpose and meaning in your life. Take each day as it comes, knowing that you have the strength and courage to navigate whatever lies ahead.

A Message of Hope

In closing, I want to leave you with a message of hope. No matter how dark the night may seem, dawn always follows. No matter how difficult the journey, there is always a path forward. Believe in yourself, in your strength, and in your ability to overcome. Hold on to hope, for it is the light that will guide you through the darkest times.

Your journey is unique, but it is also part of a larger human experience. We are all connected by our shared struggles and triumphs, our fears and hopes, our pain and joy. Together, we can create a world where mental well-being is prioritized, where everyone feels valued and supported. Let us walk this path with hope in our hearts and a commitment to embrace the journey, no matter where it leads.

Final Gratitude

To everyone who has journeyed with me through these pages, thank you. Your courage, resilience, and willingness to explore these difficult topics are inspiring. As we move forward, let us continue to support one another, to listen with empathy, and to strive for a world where mental well-being is a universal priority.

Thank you for being a part of this journey. May you find peace, joy, and fulfillment in your life. May you continue to grow, to heal, and to thrive. And may you always remember that you are not alone. Together, we can create a brighter future, one step at a time.

Embracing the Journey Ahead

As we look to the future, let us do so with a sense of hope and determination. The journey towards mental well-being is not always easy, but it is always worthwhile. Each step forward, no matter how small, is a triumph. Each moment of vulnerability, each act of resilience, each discovery of purpose and meaning brings us closer to our true selves.

Let us embrace this journey with open hearts and minds, with courage and compassion. Let us support one another, celebrate our victories, and learn from our challenges. Together, we can create a world where mental well-being is a universal priority, where everyone feels valued and supported.

Thank you for sharing this journey with me. May we continue to walk this path together, with hope in our hearts and a commitment to embrace the journey, no matter where it leads.

INDEX

- **Comorbidity**: The simultaneous presence of two or more diseases or medical conditions in a patient, such as depression and anxiety.

D

- **Dopamine**: A neurotransmitter involved in mood regulation, pleasure, and motivation, often implicated in depression.

E

- **ECT (Electroconvulsive Therapy)**: A medical treatment for severe depression involving electrically induced seizures.
- **Emotional Numbness**: A state of feeling disconnected from one's emotions, often experienced in depression.

F

- **Fatigue**: Persistent tiredness or exhaustion, commonly associated with depression.

G

- **Genetic Predisposition**: The inherited likelihood of developing depression due to genetic factors.

H

- **Hypersomnia**: Excessive sleepiness or prolonged sleep, a symptom that can accompany depression.

I

- **Insomnia**: Difficulty falling or staying asleep, often seen in individuals with depression.
- **Irritability**: Increased sensitivity to annoyance or anger, frequently observed in depression.

J

- **Journaling**: The practice of writing down thoughts and feelings, which can be therapeutic for managing depression.

L

- **Libido**: Sexual drive, which can be diminished in individuals with depression.

M

- **MDD (Major Depressive Disorder)**: A mental health disorder characterized by persistent and intense feelings of sadness for extended periods.
- **Mindfulness**: The practice of being present and fully engaged with the current moment, often used in therapies for depression.

N

- **Neurotransmitters**: Chemicals in the brain that transmit signals between nerve cells, implicated in the regulation of mood and affected in depression.

P

- **Perfectionism**: A personality trait characterized by striving for flawlessness, often contributing to depression.
- **Psychomotor Agitation**: Increased physical activity or restlessness associated with depression.
- **Psychotherapy**: A treatment approach for mental health issues involving talking to a mental health professional.

R

- **Rumination**: Repeatedly thinking about distressing situations or events, commonly seen in depression.

S

- **SSRI (Selective Serotonin Reuptake Inhibitor)**: A class of medications used to treat depression by increasing levels of serotonin in the brain.
- **Seasonal Affective Disorder (SAD)**: A type of depression that occurs at certain times of the year, usually in the winter.
- **Serotonin**: A neurotransmitter that affects mood, appetite, and sleep, often targeted in depression treatments.
- **Social Withdrawal**: The tendency to pull away from social interactions, a common symptom of depression.

T

- **Therapy**: Various treatment methods used to alleviate symptoms of depression, including CBT, ACT, and others.
- **Trauma**: Past traumatic experiences can contribute to the development of depression.

V

- **Vulnerability**: The state of being open to emotional harm, which can be a significant factor in the experience and treatment of depression.

W

- **Worthlessness**: Feelings of inadequacy and low self-worth, commonly experienced in depression.

REFERENCES & READINGS

BOOKS

Tolle, Eckhart. **The Power of Now: A Guide to Spiritual Enlightenment**. New World Library, 1997.

Sapolsky, Robert M. **Why Zebras Don't Get Ulcers: The Acclaimed Guide to Stress, Stress-Related Diseases, and Coping**. Holt Paperbacks, 2004.

Frankl, Viktor E. **Man's Search for Meaning**. Beacon Press, 1946.

Beck, Aaron T. **Cognitive Therapy and the Emotional Disorders**. International Universities Press, 1976.

Burns, David D. **Feeling Good: The New Mood Therapy**. William Morrow, 1980.

Linehan, Marsha M. **Cognitive-Behavioral Treatment of Borderline Personality Disorder**. Guilford Press, 1993.

Seligman, Martin E.P. **Learned Optimism: How to Change Your Mind and Your Life**. Vintage Books, 1991.

Kabat-Zinn, Jon. **Full Catastrophe Living: Using the Wisdom of Your Body and Mind to Face Stress, Pain, and Illness**. Delacorte Press, 1990.

Young, Jeffrey E., and Janet S. Klosko. **Reinventing Your Life: The Breakthrough Program to End Negative Behavior and Feel Great Again**. Penguin Books, 1994.

ARTICLES AND PAPERS

Beck, Aaron T., et al. "***Cognitive Therapy of Depression: New Perspectives.***" Cognitive Therapy and Research, vol. 1, no. 1, 1977, pp. 5-37.

Clark, David A., et al. "***Cognitive Mediation of Depression***." Cognitive Therapy and Research, vol. 13, no. 1, 1989, pp. 5-18.

Saxe, Glenn N., et al. "***A Trauma-Focused Approach to Treating Depression in Adolescent Refugees: A Psychotherapy Case Study***." Clinical Case Studies, vol. 7, no. 2, 2008, pp. 127-147.

WEBSITES AND ONLINE RESOURCES

- National Institute of Mental Health (NIMH) - www.nimh.nih.gov
- American Psychological Association (APA) - www.apa.org
- Mindfulness-Based Stress Reduction (MBSR) - www.mindfulnessprograms.com
- Mental Health America (MHA) - www.mhanational.org
- Psychology Today - www.psychologytoday.com

JOURNALS

- *Journal of Affective Disorders*
- *Cognitive Therapy and Research*
- *Behavior Research and Therapy*

If you or someone you know is struggling with depression or other mental health issues, it's important to seek help. Here are some resources that can provide support, information, and assistance.

CRISIS AND EMERGENCY HELP

988 Suicide & Crisis Lifeline (Previously: National Suicide Prevention Lifeline) (USA)

- **Phone**: 9-8-8 (Previously: 1-800-273-8255)
- **Website**: https://988lifeline.org/
- **Text**: HOME to 741741 (USA)

Samaritans (UK and Ireland)

- **Phone**: 116 123
- **Website**: samaritans.org

GENERAL MENTAL HEALTH SUPPORT

National Alliance on Mental Illness (NAMI)

- **Phone**: 1-800-950-NAMI (1-800-950-6264)
- **Website**: nami.org

Mental Health America (MHA)

- **Phone**: 1-800-969-6642
- **Website**: mhanational.org

Mind (UK)

- **Phone**: 0300 123 3393
- **Website**: mind.org.uk

Beyond Blue (Australia)

- **Phone**: 1300 22 4636
- **Website**: beyondblue.org.au

ONLINE THERAPY AND COUNSELING

- **BetterHelp Website**: betterhelp.com
- **Talkspace Website**: talkspace.com
- **7 Cups Website**: 7cups.com

SPECIALIZED SUPPORT

Trevor Project (LGBTQ Youth)

- **Phone**: 1-866-488-7386
- **Text**: START to 678678
- **Website**: thetrevorproject.org

Veterans Crisis Line

- **Phone**: 1-800-273-8255 (Press 1)
- **Text**: 838255
- **Website**: veteranscrisisline.net

RAINN (Rape, Abuse & Incest National Network)

- **Phone**: 1-800-656-HOPE (1-800-656-4673)
- **Website**: rainn.org

EDUCATIONAL RESOURCES

National Institute of Mental Health (NIMH)

- **Website**: nimh.nih.gov

American Psychological Association (APA)

- **Website**: apa.org

MentalHealth.gov

- **Website**: mentalhealth.gov

INTERNATIONAL RESOURCES

World Health Organization (WHO)

- **Website**: who.int/mental_health

International Association for Suicide Prevention (IASP)

- **Website**: iasp.info

Befrienders Worldwide

- **Website**: befrienders.org

COMMUNITY AND PEER SUPPORT

Depression and Bipolar Support Alliance (DBSA)

- **Phone**: 1-800-826-3632
- **Website**: dbsalliance.org

Anxiety and Depression Association of America (ADAA)

- **Website**: adaa.org

Remember, reaching out for help is a sign of strength. You are not alone, and support is available. Whether you need someone to talk to in a crisis or ongoing support, these resources can help guide you on your path to mental wellness.

Dear Reader,

Thank you from the bottom of my heart for taking the time to read "Undepressed: Navigating the Path to Mental Wellness." Writing this book was a deeply personal journey, filled with both challenges and triumphs. Sharing my story and insights with you means the world to me, and I sincerely hope it has brought you some comfort, understanding, and hope.

As an author, one of the most meaningful gifts I can receive is your feedback. Your review not only helps me improve but also aids countless others in finding this book. Reviews are vital in spreading the word and supporting mental health awareness.

If you could spare a few moments to leave a review, it would make a significant difference. Knowing that you've taken the time to share your thoughts encourages me to continue writing and advocating for mental health.

Here's why your review matters:

- It Helps Others: Your insights can guide potential readers to this book, offering them the support and understanding they might be seeking.

- It Supports the Author: Reviews are crucial for authors, especially those who write about sensitive and personal topics. Your feedback can help me reach a wider audience and continue my work.

- I'll Read Every Review: I genuinely value your feedback and take it to heart. Constructive criticism helps me grow, and your positive notes inspire me to keep going.

Thank you for being a part of this journey with me. Your support means everything.

Warm regards,

Waleed Mahmud

www.ingramcontent.com/pod-product-compliance
Lightning Source LLC
Chambersburg PA
CBHW051528150726
47997CB00001B/430